D1608929

The Flower of Paradise and
Other Armenian Tales

World Folklore Advisory Board

THE FLOWER OF PARADISE AND OTHER ARMENIAN TALES

Translated and Retold by Bonnie C. Marshall

Edited and with a Foreword by Virginia A. Tashjian

World Folklore Series

LIBRARIES
U N L I M I T E D
A Member of the Greenwood Publishing Group

Westport, Connecticut • London

Library of Congress Cataloging-in-Publication Data

Marshall, Bonnie C.
  The flower of paradise and other Armenian tales / translated and retold
  by Bonnie C. Marshall ; edited and with a foreword by Virginia Tashjian.
    p. cm. — (World folklore series)
  Includes bibliographical references and index.
  ISBN-13: 978–1–59158–367–7 (alk. paper)
  ISBN-10: 1–59158–367–5 (alk. paper)
  1. Tales—Armenia (Republic) I. Tashjian, Virginia A. II. Title.
GR277.M37 2007
  398.209566'2—dc22   2006037738

British Library Cataloguing in Publication Data is available.

Library of Congress Catalog Card Number: 2006037738
ISBN: 978-1-59158-367-7

First published in 2007

Libraries Unlimited, 88 Post Road West, Westport, CT 06881
A Member of the Greenwood Publishing Group, Inc.
www.lu.com

Printed in the United States of America

The paper used in this book complies with the
Permanent Paper Standard issued by the National
Information Standards Organization (Z39.48–1984).

10 9 8 7 6 5 4 3 2 1

All photographs, unless otherwise noted, are provided courtesy of Andranik Michaelian.

The publisher has done its best to make sure the instructions and/or recipes in this book are correct.
However, users should apply judgment and experience when preparing recipes, especially parents
and teachers working with young people. The publisher accepts no responsibility for the outcome of
any recipe included in this volume.

This book is dedicated to my youngest grandchildren, Marshall Matthews and Cooper Carey, in hopes that they will enjoy the stories when they reach the age of understanding.

It is dedicated, too, to my mother Agnes, brother Bradford, and sister-in-law Kennetha. Thanks for the memories of Scotland.

CONTENTS

Part 1: Animal Tales

Part 2: Myths and Legends

Part 3: Fairy Tales

Part 4: Tales of Everyday Life

Part 5: Wits and Dimwits

FOREWORD

Bonnie C. Marshall has retold some very wonderful old Armenian folktales under five headings: "Animal Tales," "Myths and Legends," "Fairy Tales," "Tales of Everyday Life," and "Wits and Dimwits." Each of these contains multiple stories from her research into the literature of Armenia. Each of the stories, in turn, exemplifies the gamut of emotions that Armenian folktales explore. AND I HAVE ENJOYED ENORMOUSLY READING THEM ALL!

Armenian folklore is the accumulated wisdom and art of the simple, everyday life collected by the people living in the region of the world known as Armenia. Like the stories of many other nations of the world, Armenian folklore stimulates the child's imagination. These tales will demonstrate home truths of right and wrong; they will show good versus evil learned by a sort of osmosis; they will depict what is beauty and what is truth; they will describe what is beautiful in all things; in the process, they will convey universal truths. Also, of course, they will teach us the beauty of language!

My own love for Armenian folktales started back in Brockton, Massachusetts, home of my childhood many years ago, where my younger sister Armane and I listened with open ears to the stories of my mother's youth and where her maternal Uncle Stepan told us so many improbable stories from the time of his ill-starred prison sentence.

Those stories showed us how to laugh and what to laugh at. We chuckled at Armenian common folk resolving their daily problems in a peculiar, humorous fashion. We laughed at the rollicking stories of genies and foolish men who cannot recognize good luck even when it stares them in the face! And we, certainly, learned what is acceptable and what is not.

All these stories may or may not follow a formulaic beginning and an equally formulaic ending. "Once there was and was not" is certainly as good a beginning as making the announcement, "Now, we are leaving the present to enter another realm of time or space." Any of a number of endings such as "Three apples fell from heaven: one for the teller, one for the listener, and one for all the peoples of the world" or some variant may serve as an appropriate ending. "The people lived happily ever after. May you, too, receive your heart's desire" is yet another available ending.

It is axiomatic that children are children for a very short time when we review the gamut of childhood: infancy, childhood, young adulthood, and so forth. Thus, it is imperative that they acquire the knowledge of a body of literature quickly and concisely and once and for all!

Poetic images and allusions should stock the minds of children and fill them with ethnic pride in the goodness that always prevailed over evil. They will always remember the everlasting courage of the Armenian man or woman who inevitably wins over any wicked man or beast as well as the picture of the twin peaks of Ararat.

The universality of the story is rampant in these tales of Armenians. Yes, violence there is, but wisdom and idealism are ever present as well. The clever Armenian peasant working in his fields is not much different from the Norwegian Viking crossing the fjords in his need and emotions. Truly, the tapestry of folk heritage proves the richness of the brotherhood of man.

Virginia A. Tashjian

ACKNOWLEDGMENTS

To old and new friends who spirited me on a journey through Armenian folklore and aided me along the way, I wish to extend my sincere gratitude. Serendipity played a role in my finding the people who contributed to this collection of folktales.

The manner in which I found my editor, Virginia A. Tashjian, is an example. When Ralph Di Natale, my hairdresser, learned that I was looking for an editor, he contacted clients A. P. Nichiporuk and E. A. Nichiporuk. They, in turn, led me to librarian, storyteller, and author of several volumes of Armenian folktales, Virginia A. Tashjian. "When all else fails, ask your hairdresser," Ralph quipped. I am very grateful to Virginia for her advice and conscientious scrutiny of my work.

Another fortunate discovery occurred when I was searching for a photographer and hope of finding one in the United States had grown dim. One day I chanced upon William Michaelian's Web site and asked his advice. He told me that his brother Andranik, who was living in Armenia, had quite a number of good photographs on his Web page. When I viewed Andranik Michaelian's site, it looked familiar, and I realized that almost a year before to the day I had visited it while doing research and had tucked it into the back of my mind as a possible source of photographs. Andranik Michaelian's photographs are so stunning that they received compliments from viewers long before the manuscript went into production.

Andranik's photographs were an inspiration to the talented artist Igor Karpov, who created the magical etchings for the tales. The Armenian photographer Martin Shahbazyan graciously gave permission for his stunning photograph of Mount Ararat to be used here. I was introduced to Mr. Shahbazyan by a former student, Vahe Gabrielyan, who was one of the first Soviet exchange students to study at Davidson College, where I was teaching Russian at the time. Today Vahe is a diplomat in London and was appointed Armenia's Ambassador to the Court of St. James.

Others who gave generously of time, advice, and resources include Dorothy Derapelian, who provided language primers; Zina Nikitina, who sent Armenian postcards from Russia; Virginia A. Tashjian and Gloria Derapelian, who donated recipes; cartographer Joan Garner; and Pat Bolduc, who provided information about the Armenian massacres and 1915 genocide. I am grateful to Kennetha and Bradford Marshall and to Miss Print for printing services. Last, I wish to thank the Meredith Public Library for facilitating interlibrary loan services.

INTRODUCTION

Composed of breathtaking mountains and fruitful plateaus and located south of the Caucasus Mountains in southwest Asia, Armenia has served for centuries as a buffer zone between Europe and Asia. Armenia's position on the ancient Silk Road made it vulnerable to the attacks of covetous neighbors. Throughout history, its borders have been ever changing. Overrun and controlled by Assyrians, Persians, Romans, Greeks, Mongols, Turks, and Russians, nevertheless, thanks to the bravery and indomitable spirit of its people, Armenia has survived battles, foreign rule, and genocide.

Today Armenia, which once extended from the Black to the Caspian Sea and from the Mediterranean Sea to Iran, is much reduced in size and is an independent country called the Republic of Armenia. It is 11,506 square miles (18,521 square kilometers) in area, and its capital is Yerevan.[1] It is surrounded by Georgia to the north, Iran to the south, Azerbaijan to the east, and Turkey to the west.

In addition, an enclave of Armenians lives in a region that was part of historic Armenia called Nagorno-Karabakh, which is located within and separated from present-day Armenia by Azerbaijan. In 1988 the dispute between the Nagorno-Karabakh Armenians and the Azeri Turks of Azerbaijan over this territory, which is 1,700 square miles (2,736 square kilometers) in area, erupted in a massacre of Armenians in a suburb of Baku called Sumgait. The struggle for Nagorno-Karabakh ended in an uneasy cease-fire in 1994.

Geography

Armenia, a mountainous country, has many mountains more than 10,000 feet (3,048 meters) tall. Armenia's highest mountain is Mount Aragats (also known as Mount Alagez). Mount Ararat (known to the Armenians as Masis), which is 17,000 feet (5,182 meters) high, looms over Yerevan, Armenia's capital. Once part of Armenia, the mountain now belongs to Turkey. However, Armenians consider it to be their holy mountain, and it is closely linked to their sense of identity and to their creation myth. Noah's ark is thought to have landed atop Mount Ararat, and Armenia is believed to be the cradle of humanity, the biblical Garden of Eden. Prior to the advent of Christianity, Mount Ararat was believed to be a sacred place where the sun set and where heroes were born. At the base of Mount Ararat mythical snakes and dragons were thought to live. A volcanic crater located below the mountaintop is in fact reminiscent of a dragon's lair.[2]

Mount Ararat.

Rivers include, among others, the Araks, Hrazdan, Debed, Arpa, and Vorotan. Lake Sevan (also called the Geghama Sea) is the largest lake in the Caucasus and the highest fresh-water alpine lake in the world.[3]

Armenia's landscape ranges from grass-covered steppes to meadows, forests, and deep mountain gorges. Its continental climate varies according to elevation. Summers are hot in the lowlands and cooler in the highlands. Winters are cold and snowy.

People and Labor

Historically, Armenia has been famous for its vineyards, winemaking, and horse breeding. Crops include fruits (peaches, apricots, apples, pomegranates), nuts, tobacco, and grains. For many years, Armenia's economy was largely agrarian, but under Soviet rule Armenia developed into a modern, industrialized republic.[4]

Armenia is densely populated, with population estimates ranging from a conservative 2,982,904 people in 2005 to 3,344,336 in July 2000 to 3,800,000 in 1998.[5] There appears to be a loss of population in recent years, apparently due to the post-Soviet-era exodus of Armenians. The population is homogeneous, with 93 percent being Armenian and 2 percent being Russian.[6] The remainder of the population is composed mainly of Azeris and Kurds.

Religion

The majority of Armenians (94 to 95 percent) belong to the Armenian Apostolic Church, unique and isolated from other branches of orthodoxy because of its rejection of dyophysitism (the belief that Jesus has both a human and a divine nature) as decreed by the Council of Chalcedon in AD 451. The Armenian Apostolic Church espouses instead a form of monophysitism (the belief that Jesus has a single divine nature) called miaphysitism.

Armenia was the first country to adopt Christianity as a state religion in AD 301. After surviving many years in a pit, where Tiridates had placed him for his Christian beliefs, Gregory the Illuminator converted King Tiridates III to Christianity. "The Legend about Tiridates (Trdat) III" relates the story of the suffering of Gregory, the Christian martyr, and the nuns who fell victim to Tiridates. The adoption of Christianity served to strengthen Armenia's sense of identity.

The Catholicos of all Armenians, the head of the Church, lives in Echmiadzin, where the church was established. However, because of inner conflicts and because Armenians were driven to other areas over the course of history during forced exiles, death marches, massacres, and genocide, there are four Sees in all. Besides the Supreme Catholicos at Echmiadzin, there is a Catholicos of Cilicia and two Patriarchs, one in Constantinople (Istanbul) and another in Jerusalem.

**Echmiadzin Cathedral, built in AD 480, is the oldest surviving church in Armenia.
It was constructed by King Tiridates III and Gregory the Illuminator.**

Language

Armenian represents the only surviving Thracian branch of the Indo-European languages.[7] Mesrop Mashtots, a monk and scholar, created thirty-six letters of the thirty-eight letter alphabet in AD 405. The Armenian alphabet was based largely on Greek and Aramaic characters.[8]

Statue in Echmiadzin commemorating Mesrop Mashtots,
inventor of the Armenian alphabet.

The Armenian language contains many words borrowed from Greek, Aramaic, Turkish, Persian, and Russian. Three forms of the language exist today: Classical Armenian (Grabar) is the scholarly language used by the Church, Western Armenian is used in the Diaspora, and Eastern Armenian is the spoken language and the official language of the Republic of Armenia.

The invention of an alphabet ushered in a Golden Age of literature and intellectual growth. After liturgical and historical documents were translated into Armenian, scholars had ready access to the Bible and to valuable medieval religious, historical, medical, and philosophical works. Indeed, books are so highly regarded by Armenians that the medieval belief in "saint books" as talismans capable of protecting their possessors is still found.

"Saint books" are covered in cloth, placed in a box, and brought out only when needed to resolve a problem.[9]

History

Armenia's history has been turbulent and complex. The Armenian name for Armenia is Hayastan, and the Armenians themselves are Hay. Hayk was the name of Armenia's ancestral hero who won a decisive battle over Bel, the Assyrian giant reminiscent of the Old Testament Goliath. Hayk's name provided the root seen in the Armenian words for the country and the people.

Origins and Ancient History

Hamlet Petrosyan outlines two theories regarding the origin of the Armenians. The first is that they originated in the area between the Black Sea and Lake Van, which is located today in eastern Turkey. The second theory is that the Armenians migrated from the Balkans to Anatolia (Turkey) in the second millennium BC.[10] At any rate, the presence of Armenians during the rule of the powerful kingdom of Urartu has been recorded. However, in the eighth century BC Urartu was invaded by Scythians. Armenians replaced the Urartians as rulers, and the kingdom became part of Medea, which was located in present-day Iran. Persia's Achaemenid Empire (550–330 BC) conquered Medea, and the Armenians fell under Persian influence. It was during this era that Armenians became known for their skill in winemaking and horse breeding.[11]

A new Greek influence came with the invasion of Alexander the Great, or Alexander of Macedon, who conquered the Persians in 331 BC. Under Greek influence, the Armenian gods took on Greek characteristics.[12] Not all of Armenia fell to Alexander. The north remained free. Even after the Seleucids (Syrians) replaced Alexander upon his death in 323 BC, Greek influence remained strong.

In 189 BC the Roman Empire conquered the Seleucian Empire, and Armenia was divided into two provinces, Greater and Lesser Armenia. The northern section of Armenia declared its independence. Artashes (Artaxias) of the Artashesian Dynasty (189 BC–AD 10) ruled Greater Armenia, which reached the height of its power under the rule of Tigranes or Tigran (Dikran) the Great (95–55 BC). Tigranes expanded Armenia's territories greatly. His capital city, Tigranakert, became a Greek intellectual center. Sadly, Tigranes the Great failed to repel the Romans and Parthians, and in 66 BC Tigranes the Great lost a great deal of his territory to the Romans.[13] Tigranes' country served as a buffer between the Romans and the Persian Parthians, who were later replaced by the Persian Sassanid Dynasty and Greek Byzantium.

The Christian Era

Of the series of dynasties following the Artashesian, the Arsacid Dynasty (AD 52–428) of the Armenians stands out and survived.[14] With the adoption of Christianity by the Arsacid King Tiridates III in AD 301, Armenia's sense of identity as the first Christian state was in place. National pride was strengthened with the invention of an alphabet and the church's refusal to accept dyophysitism, as had the other Orthodox churches. From then on Armenia was oriented more toward the West and began distancing itself from the East and the Persian Zoroastrian Sassanids, who differed in religious beliefs.

In AD 387 Byzantium and Persia divided Armenia, most of which fell to Persia. The Persians ruled through the selection of native Armenian princes, called *nakharas*, until the seventh century, when the Persian Sassanid Dynasty fell and Persian Armenia came under Arab control in AD 653.

The Armenian Bagratid Dynasty (AD 884–1045) was established under Ashot V. However, it became fragmented because it was unable to prevent independent princes from creating other kingdoms within Armenia. Nevertheless, under King Gagik Bagratuni I (AD 989–1020) there was a Golden Age of culture and business.

Turkish and Mongol Rule

The weakened Byzantine Empire managed to gain control of Armenia, but Byzantium was conquered in 1071 by the Seljuk Turks, who in turn invaded Armenia and won control of it. The Seljuk Turks exterminated wealthy intellectual Armenians.

Many Armenians moved south to Cilicia in Byzantium to join those resettled in Syria and Cilicia earlier by Byzantium. These Armenians formed the Rubenid Dynasty and the Armenian State of Cilicia (AD 1080–1375), which is also called Lesser Armenia. They were exposed to European culture, especially during the Crusades. After Mongols descended on the land in 1375, Cilicia became part of the Egyptian Mamluk Kingdom and was not free again until the modern era.

Armenia was ruled by the Ottoman Empire and Persia after the death of the Mongol leader Tamerlane in 1405. After the fall of Constantinople to the Turks in 1453, the Turkish sultan created an Armenian See in Constantinople, so the center of Armenian religious and political affairs shifted to Constantinople in the Turkish Ottoman Empire. Prosperous Armenians were separated literally and figuratively from Armenians living in Cilicia and Anatolia. In 1828 Persian Armenia became part of the Russian Empire.

Massacres, Genocide, and the Diaspora

Sultan Abdul-Hamid II (1876–1909), fearful of Armenian nationalism that was upheld by Russia, ordered a series of massacres from 1894 to 1896. Thousands were killed. Estimates range from 100,000 to 300,000.[15] Although Armenians were hopeful that the Young Turks' revolution of 1908 would bring reform, the massacres resumed. When Armenians espoused the Allied side during World War I (1914–1918) and joined the Russians in fighting the Turks, the Turkish government exiled 1,750,000 Armenians to the Syrian Desert in a death march. Loss of life has been estimated from 600,000 to 1,500,000.[16] In an attempt at total genocide, the Turks burned and destroyed everything the Armenians had left behind in their villages. Unable to return home, Armenians moved to other countries, such as Russia, France, and the United States, and formed a Diaspora. The Armenians who fled to Russia settled in a small section of historic Armenia.

The Soviet Era and Modern Armenia

In 1916 Armenia, Azerbaijan, and Georgia formed a brief Transcaucasian union. Equally brief was an independent Armenian republic formed in 1920. In 1922 Armenia had little choice but to join Georgia and Azerbaijan to become the Transcaucasian Soviet Federated Socialist Republic as part of the Union of Soviet Socialist Republics. Armenia gained the status of republic in 1936.

From 1921 to 1991 Armenia was controlled by the Soviet Union. Although the Russians had come to Armenia's aid against the Turks, Armenians were not blind to the shortcomings of the Soviet government. At a time when people were being imprisoned for up to ten years for telling jokes critical of the regime, a cycle of "Radio Yerevan," or "Radio Armenia," jokes were circulating in Moscow and in large urban centers of the Soviet Union. Attributed to Armenian wit, "Radio Yerevan" jokes satirized the philosophy of Marxism and the social injustices of the Soviet system. The joke below is credited with giving birth to the entire "Radio Yerevan" cycle.[17]

> We (Radio Yerevan) were asked, "How does communism differ from capitalism?"
>
> We replied, "Under capitalism mankind exploited mankind, but under communism it is just the opposite."

Even before the Soviet Union fell, Armenia had plans to seek independence. In 1991, independence was declared.

Economic and political problems persist today. Corruption and graft, which accompanied the fall of the Soviet Union, have left Armenian voters disillusioned and alienated. In 1988 an earthquake struck northwestern Armenia, killing from 25,000 to 55,000 people and destroying several cities, including Gyumri and Spitak. Armenia is still recovering from this event. The Nagorno-Karabakh issue is hardly resolved, and fighting could erupt again to disrupt the economy and the operation of the Caspian Sea oil fields. In 1999 five gunmen held Parliament hostage and killed several officials, bringing about a government crisis. During this incident, information was not disseminated and reporters were arrested. In 2002 President Robert Kocharian's bodyguard killed a Georgian Armenian in a Yerevan restaurant and got off lightly for the murder. The fairness of elections continues to be scrutinized and questioned by international monitors.[18]

The miracle is that Armenia managed to survive throughout its turbulent history, that it resisted the domination of nation after nation and overcame disasters, wars, and genocide. Somehow, throughout the ordeal, Armenians managed to preserve their quick wit and retain their brave and resilient spirit.

Armenian Life

Armenian hospitality is fabled. Armenians are a sociable, gregarious people who take pride in their traditions and enjoy good fellowship and celebratory events. Fortunately, their dark history has failed to dampen their spirits. Religious and secular holidays provide an opportunity for the gathering of family and friends.

Religious holidays include Christmas, Palm Sunday, Easter, Purification, St. Sargis Day, the Transfiguration, St. Mary's Day, Day of the Holy Cross, and Ascension Day. Many religious holidays usurped pagan holidays and were purposely established on the same day.[19]

Christmas is celebrated on January 6 in accordance with the Orthodox calendar. The birth of Christ and his baptism in the River Jordan, commemorated in the blessing of water, are observed on that day. In pagan times the birth of the sun was celebrated in December, so Christmas, which comes soon after in January, replaces a pagan holiday. Armenians attend church services on Christmas Eve and Christmas morning. Afterward a family feast, often of fish and rice, is shared.

On St. Sargis Day, observed between January 18 and February 23, historically young men and women ate salty food and drank a great deal of water to engender dreams of their future wives and husbands. In hopes of seeing the lucky hoof print of St. Sargis' horse, they placed a dish of flour outside their doors.

On February 14, forty days after Christ's birth, the Purification (*Trndez*) is observed. A bonfire is lit to symbolize coming to Christ with fire. Beneath this Christian layer is an ancient pagan celebration of the advent of spring.

Vardanants is a religious feast that takes place on the Thursday preceding Lent in memory of Vardan Mamikonian (AD 400–451), who lost his life defending the Christian Armenians against the Persian Zoroastrians, who wanted the Armenians to relinquish Christianity in favor of Zoroastrianism.

Palm Sunday (*Tsaghkazard*), which commemorates Christ's coming to Jerusalem as the Savior, is observed a week before Easter. Easter (*Zatik*) is the most beloved holiday. Legend has it that when Christ was crucified, His mother Mary brought Him eggs and bread (*choereg*) wrapped in a shawl. When she saw her Son bleeding, she cried. Christ's blood and His mother's tears fell on the shawl, eggs, and bread, and turned them red. In observance of this incident, women wear shawls to church and eggs are colored red.

Ascension Day, which is in May, commemorates Christ's ascent to heaven. It was established to replace an ancient celebration of spring, during which young people strolled and made new friends. The former celebration included a night of miracles when nature spoke and magic events were witnessed.

The Transfiguration (*Vardavar*) is a summer holiday observed in June or July. In Armenian mythology Astghik, goddess of love, beauty, and water, spread love by sprinkling rose water and roses throughout the land. In Astghik's honor, Armenians distribute roses and sprinkle water on one another. Today *Vardavar* has been remade into a Christian holiday.

Vardavar **holiday celebrating the Transfiguration of Christ**
at Haghardzin Monastery.

Between August 12 and 18, St. Mary's Day is celebrated. It is a harvest festival that includes the yearly blessing of the grapes in church. During the Day of the Holy Cross in September, the dead are remembered and commemorated.

Secular holidays include New Year, Women's Day, Motherhood and Beauty Day, Genocide Victims' Memorial Day, First Republic Day, Constitution Day, Independence Day, May 9th Victory Day, and Earthquake Victims' Memorial Day.

The New Year's celebration, which is observed on January 1, actually lasts a week. Armenians bake for the New Year (*Amanor*) to prepare for guests. People come by to wish the hosts well and to exchange gifts. *Dzmer Papik*, who resembles our Santa Claus, brings gifts to the children.

There are two holidays devoted to women. On March 8, International Women's Day, men present all women with gifts and flowers. In addition to Women's Day, Motherhood and Beauty Day is observed on April 7. Similar to our Mother's Day, on that day mothers are given flowers and gifts.

Victims of the 1915 genocide are honored on April 24 during Genocide Victims' Memorial Day. Respect is paid to more than a million victims of the attempt by the Turkish government to exterminate the Armenians. To this day Turkey denies this event, dubbing it a civil war rather than genocide.

Three holidays are connected to statehood. On May 28, First Republic Day, Armenians celebrate the establishment of the short-lived 1918 republic. Constitution Day commemorates the adoption of a constitution for the Republic of Armenia on July 5, 1995. Independence Day, which is celebrated on September 21, observes the reestablishment of the Republic of Armenia in 1991 after seventy years of Soviet rule. Another holiday connected to Soviet rule is the May 9th Victory Day, which commemorates the end of World War II.

Earthquake Victims' Memorial Day on December 7 is dedicated to the memory of the victims of the 1988 earthquake that decimated Armenia's infrastructure.

Armenians value family traditions. Although family traditions may appear to be dated in today's modern world, these traditions have made it possible for Armenians to preserve their culture and ethnicity, despite the challenges they have faced historically. Armenians tend to marry other Armenians, and marriage between people of the same region who share the same values is considered ideal. Women marry young and adhere to a strict code of conduct. A woman stands when a man enters the room, shows respect for her husband, and cares for the house and children. Men, too, are supposed to show respect for their wives. The oldest male is the head of the household and maintains order. Children are deferential to adults, and relatives are important in their upbringing, especially uncles, for whom children have a high regard.[20]

Traditional dress for men consisted of a shirt and baggy trousers, over which a caftan and fur coat were worn. A lamb's fur hat was worn atop the head. Women wore brocade, silk, or satin dresses, over which they wore a caftan and sleeveless jacket, which revealed beautifully embroidered sleeves. Jewelry (silver bracelets and anklets, head ornaments, necklaces, and nose jewelry) was especially valued and was passed down from generation to generation.[21]

Boy and girl dressed in traditional attire.

The poetic nature of the Armenian people is apparent in their applied arts. In addition to creating the jewelry described above, craftsmen from the Bronze Age to the present have shown an interest in metalwork. Swords, daggers, gun butts, and powder flasks have been adorned with precious metals and jewels. Manuscripts and books, so revered by Armenians, were preserved with gold and silver bindings and were illuminated with paintings and decorations. Armenians are master carpet weavers. They cover floors, walls, trunks, and beds with carpets. The oldest design is the dragon-rug (*Vishapakagh*). You may recall that Mount Ararat was the fabled abode of dragons. Later, the tree-of-life carpet design became popular.[22]

The Tales

History of Armenian Folklore

Armenia's role as a buffer state between East and West determined the uniqueness of its folklore and culture, which embodies traits of the cultures of surrounding and invading countries. *Hekiats* (the Armenian word for folktales) were passed on by word of mouth for many generations.

After Mesrop Mashtots developed the Armenian alphabet in AD 405, folklore was recorded and preserved by the religious community. Chroniclers and historians began including folklore disguised as history, or fact, in their writings. Moses of Khoren's fifth-century *History of the Armenians* is an example. His text includes legends, myths, and folktales as well as descriptions of the folksingers known as *ashugs*.

An interest in folklore and its collection blossomed in Armenia, as it did in Europe, during the time of the Romantic Movement. Romanticism of the eighteenth and nineteenth centuries engendered in people a sense of national pride, emphasizing as it did the importance of national identity. However, it should be noted that genocide took its toll on western Armenian tellers, with the result that much of the tradition has been lost with the loss of the folk. Eastern Armenia, on the other hand, has been affected by industrialization, so that tale-telling traditions have changed there.[23]

The father of Armenian folklore was Bishop Garegin Servantsian (1840–1892).[24] He might be compared to the Brothers Grimm in Germany or Afanasev in Russia. He transcribed the heroic epic, "David of Sassoun." He also published some faithful renditions of folktales in *Tasty-Fragrant* (*Hamov-Hotov*, 1884).[25]

Sargis Haykuni (1838–1908) was a teacher who collected folktales and other folklore, which were published in the *Eminian Ethnographic Collection.*[26] Less true to the original were the tales of Hovhannes Toumanian (1869–1923), who wrote literary renditions. However, Toumanian did much to popularize folktales.

Tigran Navasardian (1861–1927) lived in poverty and traveled on foot to collect tales. He published ten volumes of *Armenian Folk Tales* and supervised forty field workers.

It was Grigor Khalatian (1858–1912) who first wrote a guide for collectors of folklore. Mkrtich Emin (1815–1890) of Moscow's Lazarian Institute for the Study of Oriental Languages encouraged Khalatian to study Armenian history and literature at the Institute. Later, Khalatian taught Armenian literature at the Institute and edited the *Eminian Ethnographic Collection.*

Ervand Lalayan (1864–1931), who was also a teacher, collected folklore using Khalatian's principles for collecting. He founded both the *Ethnographic Review* and the Armenian Ethnographic Society. Lalayan led folklore expeditions under the umbrella of the Ethnographic Society and published three volumes of folktales, entitled *Pearls.*

More recent achievements include those of Aram T. Ghanalanian (1909–1983), who compiled a bibliography of folklore. It was only in 1959 that a series of *Armenian Folk Tales* began appearing.

The Golden Maiden (1898) by A. G. Seklemian was the first collection of Armenian folktales published in English. Other collections available in English include Charles Downing's *Armenian Folk-tales and Fables* (1972); Susie Hoogasian-Villa's *100 Armenian Tales and Their Folkloristic Relevance* (1966), collected from emigrants living in Detroit; I. Khatchatrianz's *Armenian Folk Tales* (1946); Leon Surmelian's *Apples of Immortality: Folktales of Armenia* (1968); and Virginia A. Tashjian's *Once There Was and Was Not: Armenian Tales Retold* (1966) and *Three Apples Fell from Heaven: Armenian Folk Tales Retold* (1971).

Classification, Selection, and Style of Folktales

The division of folktales into three types—animal tales, fairy tales (*märchen*), and tales of everyday life, a system invented by Russian scholars—has been utilized in this book because of its convenience and because many of the sources used were Russian. In addition, a part containing myths and legends has been included. Myths and legends reveal a great deal about the values, beliefs, and rituals of a cultural group. The part entitled "Tales of Everyday Life" contains didactic stories about negative character traits, such as greed and laziness, and tales illustrative of homilies about correct behavior. The final part, entitled "Wits and Dimwits," contains narratives in which the hero is a fool or a wise man, and sometimes both, such as the folk character named Silly Pugi. The creation of a special section for tales of this type seemed quite appropriate because Armenian wit is rich and fabled and there are many tales that fall into this category.

Many classical folktales were selected because they have been loved and told and re-told for generations. "The Customer and the Hatter," "The Snake and the Fish," and "The Wolf and the Lamb," for example, have long been standard fare for elementary school reading in Soviet and post-Soviet schools in Russia.

Other stories were selected because they are interesting versions of tales that exist in other countries as well, such as "The Council of Mice" (Type 110: "Belling the Cat" in Stith Thompson's translation and enlargement of Antii Aarne's *The Types of the Folktale*), which appears in Russian, Finnish, Estonian, Irish, Italian, Hungarian, Greek, and Turkish variants.[27] "The Wolf and the Lamb" (Type 122C), in which the lamb persuades the wolf to sing, is also in Danish, Spanish, Serbian and Croatian, Greek, and Indian versions. "The Fox Who Was Deceived," in which a fox is foiled in his attack on a rooster by a dog (a variant of Type 130A), is also in Baltic and Finnish cultures. Of the fairy tales, "Okhik" (a combination of Types 325 and 313A), in which the magician or devil's daughter aids the shape-shifting hero in his escape from the girl's father, is extant in German, Baltic, Finnish, Irish, Danish, Italian, Slovenian, Serbian and Croatian, Polish, Russian, Greek, and Turkish versions, too.

Of course, Type 300 ("The Dragon-Slayer"), in which a maiden is rescued, is at the heart of fairy tales in many cultures and pertains to "Little Bear." Type 403V, in which the true bride is replaced with a false bride, is the basis of "The Extraordinary Cucumber," a tale found in Finnish, Swedish, Norwegian, Irish, French, German, Tuscan, Sicilian, Slovenian, Czech, and even African cultures. "Beauty and the Beast" (Type 425C) can be discerned in the myth entitled "The Flower of Paradise," in which a father loses his daughter to a monster because the father plucks a flower that the daughter requested. This tale type can be found in German, Baltic, Finnish, Italian, and Slavic countries. Of the tales of everyday life, which includes the section on wits and dimwits, "The Master and the Hired Man" is a variant of Type 1000 ("The Bargain Not to Become Angry"). This tale of the oppressed worker outwitting his cruel and greedy master is found in Baltic and Nordic, as well as in Scottish, Irish, French, Spanish, German, Slavic, Greek, and Turkish sources. There are many other such examples. The tales selected here offer an interesting rendition of commonly shared themes.

Some stories are unique to Armenia. Examples include many of the legends, such as the tale about Mesrop Mashtots entitled "Blazing a Trail," the story of Armenia's Christianization entitled "The Legend about Tiridates (Trdat) III," and the cycle of tales about the wise fool, Silly Pugi.

The language and style of Armenian folktales are intriguing because Armenians have a liking for wit and verbal play. There are many Armenian dialects, and the language is rich in borrowings from other languages with which the Armenians came in contact, including Russian, Turkish, and Persian.

Epithets are common. "King's son" is used instead of "prince," and "king's daughter" is used instead of "princess," in folklore texts. Formulas are repeated. "Neither a bird on the wing nor a snake on its belly would be so bold as to force its way through to this part of the world" is an example found in both "Little Bear" and "Forty Thieves." Another formula is: "Whether they traveled a long or short time, only God knows." Frequently, the disclaimer appears: "Whether it happened or not . . . " or "there was and there wasn't . . . " ("The Tailless Fox," for example). Weddings are typically celebrated for "seven days and seven nights." The most charming formulas are the ending formulas. Many are a variation on the ending formula of "Okhik": "Three apples fell from heaven—one apple for the storyteller, the second for the person listening to the story, and the third for the whole, wide world." Another common ending formula appears in "Forty Thieves": "They attained their happiness. May you attain your happiness, too."

A common feature of tale-telling style is the generous use of dialogue that enhances the dramatic effect of the story. This is particularly true of the animal tales and tales of everyday life. Detailed descriptions are lacking, even in the fairy tales, because the tale context was well known to the listener, who had no need of elaboration. I have added information to the tales only when necessary for comprehension. There is no literary enhancement.

The reader will find Armenian words italicized, unless it is a name, place name, body of water, or mountain. The English translation of that word is often then in parentheses; for example, *lumma* (penny). If an English equivalent is used, the Armenian word is in parentheses; for example, Mount Ararat (Masis). There is great variation in the spelling of translated words. In general, I used the spelling I came upon most commonly in sources. No single system was applied.

Animal Tales

Animal tales are allegories with animals, instead of human beings, as heroes. Satirical with a didactic goal, animal tales are connected to ancient beliefs about animals. Vladimir Anikin claims that animal tales date back to a time when tribes believed in animal ancestry and protection.[28] Animal tales are short, concise, and liberal with dialogue and repetition. The repetition is especially noticeable in chain stories, with their accumulating additions, such as "The Tailless Fox."

Leon Surmelian lists the horse, snake, and fox as the most popular characters in Armenian animal tales.[29] Three of the nine animal tales selected are about foxes. There is the above-mentioned tailless fox who must perform a series of tasks to get her tail back, the fox who intends to eat a rooster until she is sent to consult with the dog ("The Fox Who Was Deceived"), and the fox with little knowledge who puts the prideful and knowledgeable fox to shame ("Two Foxes"). Other animals in this collection include the snake ("The Snake and the Fish"), mice ("The Council of Mice"), and the frog ("The Avenging Frog"). The rooster ("The Invincible Rooster") , the sparrow in the story by the same name, and the lamb ("The Wolf and the Lamb") are trickster figures who outwit their predators.

Myths and Legends

Myths, which relate to a people's belief system, were told by elders to pass on information to the young, thereby perpetuating cultural values and rituals. Myths create an orderly world, in which life and nature are explained. Subjects include stories about gods and the origin of the world and of natural phenomena. For example, "Seven Stars" explains the origin of a constellation. The tale entitled "Snake Child Otsamanuk and Arevamanuk, Who Angered the Sun" is peopled by mythical heavenly bodies, as well as by Louise, Queen of the World. Other ancient gods, the Sun Maiden and the Fire Spirit, are characters in the story by the same name, which explains how the sun and fire originated. The Armenians' first god was Ar, which means the sun and is the root found in Mount Ararat's name and in the name of Armenia itself. "The Flower of Paradise," which contains a mixture of fairy-tale and mythic elements, offers an explanation for the changing of the seasons. "How God Taught the Greedy Priest a Lesson" is an Armenian version of the King Midas myth.

Legends are told as if they described real events, and often there is some basis in fact for legends. There are legends about actual religious and historical figures, although the details of the event described may be imaginary or exaggerated. For example, "Blazing a Trail" relates how the historical Mesrop Mashtots, inventor of the alphabet, built a cathedral. "The Legend about Tiridates (Trdat) III" describes the sufferings of Saints Gregory the Illuminator, Hripsimé, and Gayané during the reign of Tiridates and prior to his acceptance of Christianity in AD 301. The historical Tamerlane is the antihero of "The Mirror," and King Alexander resolves a dispute in "The Blacksmith, the Carpenter, and the Farmer."

Pourquoi, or explanatory, tales explain the origin or characteristics of a natural phenomenon. "Why the Onion Is Bitter" is a *pourquoi* tale, interesting because the hardy plantain of the story, which survives against all odds, seems to be a symbol of the Armenian people, who historically have struggled and overcome all adversities.

Fairy Tales

Fairy tales are also called wondertales and *märchen*. The plot takes place in a fantastic world, where a hero or heroine must undergo tasks, tests, or battles. Inevitably, the hero or heroine overcomes adversity, and good triumphs over evil.

The array of Armenian fairy-tale characters is rich and colorful. The totemic Little Bear in the tale by the same name is a clumsy troublemaker with extraordinary strength. Several tales are peopled with *devs*, ancient spirits variously thought to be monsters, serpents, and giants. In "Dzheiran-ogly, the Deer's Son," for example, the Maiden with Forty Braids is abducted by the White Dev.

Kings set challenges for the hero and serve as impediments, but kings either lose in battle or are outwitted by the fairy-tale hero. Little Bear, for example, wins the bride of the King of Frangistan.

Okhik, in the story of the same name, is a water spirit and shape-shifting sorcerer who plots the death of his apprentice. Other shape-shifters include the frog of "Gambar" and the cucumber maiden who transforms into a bird and a spoon in the tale "The Extraordinary Cucumber." The envious and thieving wife of the *melik* (ruler of one of Armenia's five principalities), the beloved *ashug* (folksinger), the uneducable and incompetent son, and the old woman who plays surrogate mother to the hero or heroine are stock characters.

Peris are beautiful spirits descended from evil angels. They have a dual nature and are sometimes evil and sometimes helpful. For example, the *peri* sisters of "Forty Thieves" initially test, then help, the hero.

Snakes appear frequently in fairy tales. There are the black (evil) and white (good) snakes of "The Peasant's Son and the King's Daughter." Shakmar the Snake, who battles Dzheiran-ogly and turns him to stone, is an example of a snake in an evil role.

Magic objects are common to fairy tales. They include magic wands that bring back life, pomegranates that contain jewels, as well as magic tablecloths, gourds, and rings. The fez of invisibility, the moneymaking tobacco pouch, and the fife that summons an army are magic objects that appear in "The Peasant's Son and the King's Daughter."

Even human beings and animals can have magic powers that are put in service of the hero. Examples include the Runner, the Miller, the Drinker, the Sage, the *Ashug* (folksinger), and the Strong Man who come to the aid of Little Bear. In "The Beardless Sorcerer and the King's Son," a clever mouse steals the magic ring from the mouth of the villain Beardless as he sleeps.

Tales of Everyday Life

Tales of everyday life deal with ordinary life and ordinary objects. I have chosen tales that have an emphasis on proper behavior. They address a human character flaw. Tales of everyday life are social satires that expose social injustices and human failings and support the downtrodden with a twist of humor and wit.

The good Samaritan of "The Good Deed," for example, so pesters the man he had helped with his demands for gratitude that the vexed recipient of his services undoes everything in order to be rid of his debt of gratitude. Three tales address the flaws of greed and stinginess. In "The Customer and the Hatter," a greedy customer ends up with several smaller versions of his original order. A man frugal to a fault takes his pants off so that he won't wear them out in "The Search for a *Lumma* (Penny)." A pitcher of gold becomes a pitcher of snakes when a greedy king attempts to take the gold away from the men who rightfully earned it ("The Pitcher of Gold").

Laziness, another negative trait, is the downfall of the capable lad who barely escapes the king's ire in "The Tale about a Lazy Man." Lazy Hoory in the tale of the same name requires her mother's wit to hide her lazy nature from her husband. The most extreme laziness of all is displayed by Lazy Tiuni and Uri the Slug, who would rather be buried alive than work.

In "Know-It-All Tangik," Tangik's neighbor punishes her for her prideful overconfidence by giving ridiculous directions for making stuffed grape leaves (*dolma*). In "Don't Overstay Your Visit," the reader is reminded of the old proverb that states: "Guests and fish stink after three days." "You Reap What You Sow" is an illustration of the proverb that provides its title.

Wits and Dimwits

This part contains stories about fools, clever people, and tricksters. This genre glorifies cleverness and cunning. In these tales, the scapegoat wins, and the foolish get what they deserve. Although these tales could have been included in tales of everyday life, Armenian wit is so prolific and sharp that the stories deserved special emphasis in a section of their own.

The slippery subjects of "The Shoemaker's Debt" and "When My Heart Tells Me" avoid paying their debts. The heroes of "The Golden Apple," "The Master and the Hired Man," and "Death or Freedom" are poor, but clever. They include a poor man who outwits the king, a worker who forces his cruel and greedy master to pay him and his brother for their work, and a servant who outwits a master plotting his death.

There are some dull-witted folk who can't be helped. Their foolishness leads to disaster. Such a person is the peasant in "The Donkey That Swallowed the Moon," who imagines that his donkey is responsible for the disappearance of the moon. The silly husband and wife of "Carnival" lose their store of food to a crafty stranger. An entire village of simpletons ends up doing great harm with an ax in "Brother Ax." The king's eldest son in "The Ne'er-Do-Well Son" is so senseless that when God grants him good fortune, he lets it slip through his fingers. Foolishness reaches its height in "A Tall, Tall Tale," in which the most extraordinary and absurd events occur, including a nut tree growing on a goose's back.

A series of tales about Armenia's folk hero, Silly Pugi, are included. Silly Pugi is a trickster figure who cleverly plays the fool and thereby outwits the unsuspecting. He is similar to Nasredin Hodja in Central Asian tales, Clever Peter in South Slavic tales, Shish in Russian tales, and Till Eulenspiegel in German tales. The actual Silly Pugi is said to have been born in 1713 in Avetaranots. He was a servant of the Karabakh landowner, *Melik* Shakhnazar, and his job was to entertain *Melik* Shakhnazar and his guests. He died in 1815.[30]

Armenian folktales were uniquely influenced by Armenia's neighbors and the conquerors, from whom they borrowed freely, all the while retaining a strong national identity. This identity is clearly reflected in the folktales that appear in this collection. To become familiar with them is to embark on a magical journey into the heart and soul of a proud people who have amazing survival skills and who remain undaunted by misfortune.

Notes

1. Dates and statistics referred to in this introduction are from *The Encyclopedia Americana* (International Edition 2001), *The New Encyclopaedia Britannica* (15th edition), and the *The World Almanac and Book of Facts 2005*. Discrepancies in information are noted.

2. See Hamlet Petrosyan, "The Sacred Mountain," in *Armenian Folk Arts, Culture, and Identity*, ed. Levon Abrahamian and Nancy Sweezy (Bloomington and Indianapolis: Indiana University Press, 2001), 33–39.

3. *American University of Armenia: Republic of Armenia.* Available at http://www. aua-mirror.com/aua/faculty/info1.htm (accessed January 23, 2005).

4. There is a wide discrepancy in estimates of the agricultural labor force, ranging from 7 percent in "Armenia, Republic of," in *The Encyclopedia Americana* (International Edition 2001) to 45 percent in "Armenia: Republic of Armenia," in *The World Almanac and Book of Facts 2005*.

5. Estimates given respectively in "Armenia, Republic of," in *The World Almanac and Book of Facts 2005;* "Armenia," in *Map Quest: World Atlas* (Available at http://www. mapquest.com, accessed April 5, 2006); and *Geography: Merriam-Webster's Atlas* (Available at http://www.m-w.com, accessed April 5, 2006).

6. "Armenia: Republic of Armenia," in *The World Almanac and Book of Facts 2005*.

7. "Armenia," in *The Encyclopedia Americana* (International Edition 2001).

8. Aramaic was a Semitic language used throughout the Near East from 300 BC to AD 650.

9. See a photograph of a "saint book" in Hamlet Petrosyan, "Writing and the Book," in *Armenian Folk Arts, Culture, and Identity*, ed. Levon Abrahamian and Nancy Sweezy (Bloomington and Indianapolis: Indiana University Press, 2001), 59.

10. For a clear account of Armenia's origins and ancient history, see Hamlet Petrosyan, "In the Beginning," in *Armenian Folk Arts, Culture, and Identity*, ed. Levon Abrahamian and Nancy Sweezy (Bloomington and Indianapolis: Indiana University Press, 2001).

11. See Hamlet Petrosyan, "In the Beginning," 14.

12. For a listing of the Armenian gods and their Greek counterparts, see *Tour Armenia: The Armenian Gods*. Available at http://www.tacentral.com/mythology.asp?story_no=2 (accessed March 29, 2006). Gods include Aramazd (Zeus), Anahit (Artemis), Nuneh (Athena), Vahagan (Hephaestus), Astghik (Aphrodite), and Tir (Apollo). A table of equivalent Roman, Greek, and Persian gods and their roles is given in Arra S. Avakian, *Armenia: A Journey Through History* (Fresno, CA: Electric Press, 1998–2000), 92.

13. Parthia was a country in southwest Asia, southeast of the Caspian Sea.

14. For tables of the complex and frequently confusing succession of kings and dynasties, consult Agop J. Hacikyan, ed., *The Heritage of Armenian Literature: From the Oral Tradition to the Golden Age*, vol. 1 (Detroit: Wayne State University Press, 2000), Appendix 1, 373–80; and Arra S. Avakian, *Armenia: A Journey Through History*, 67–68.

15. See Rouben Adalian, "The Armenian Genocide: Context and Legacy," *Social Education* (February 1991): 99.

16. "Armenian Massacres," in *The New Encyclopedia Britannica* (15th edition), and Rouben Adalian, "The Armenian Genocide: Context and Legacy," 102, respectively.

17. From the author's private collection. Nikolai Olin, author of *Govorit "Radio Yerevan"* (Brazzavil-Munich: Samizdat, 1970), claims that the question posed in this ancestor of "Radio Yerevan" jokes actually was posed to the chief editor of Radio Yerevan. See page 7.

18. For an analysis of the present situation in Armenia, see *The Third Republic: Glasnost to Present*. Available at http://www.tacentral.com/history_story.asp?story_no+18 (accessed March 29, 2006).

19. To learn more about Armenia's holidays, see *About Armenia: The Holidays*. Available at http://www.armeniainfo.am/about/?section=holidays (accessed January 23, 2005).

20. See *MayrHayreniq: Armenian Family*. (Site currently under construction.) Available soon at http://www.mayrhayreniq.uk.tt/ (accessed November 11, 2006).

21. See *MayrHayreniq: Armenian National Costume*. (Site currently under construction.) Available soon at http://www.mayrhayreniq.uk.tt/ (accessed November 11, 2006). For illustrations and more information, see Svetlana Poghosyan, "Costume," in *American Folk Arts, Culture, and Identity* (Bloomington and Indianapolis: Indiana University Press, 2001), 177–93.

22. For detailed descriptions and illustrations of artifacts in wood, clay, and copper, and of carpets, needle arts, costumes, and jewelry, see Levon Abrahamian and Nancy Sweezy, eds. *Armenian Folk Arts, Culture, and Identity* (Bloomington and Indianapolis: Indiana University Press, 2001).

23. It is for these reasons that Leon Surmelian mentions in his introduction to *Apples of Immortality: Folktales of Armenia* (Berkeley and Los Angeles: University of California Press, 1968), 14, that most of the tales in his book are from eastern Armenia.

24. Information regarding the most important contributors to Armenian folklore can be found in Anne M. Avakian, introduction, in *Armenian Folklore Bibliography*. University of California Publications: Catalogs and Bibliographies, 11 (Berkeley, Los Angeles, and London: University of California Press, 1994); Leon Surmelian, introduction, in *Apples of Immortality*; and G. O. Karapetian, comp. and trans., *Armianskii fol'klor* (Moscow: Nauka, Glavnaia redaktsiia vostochnoi literatury, 1979).

25. A few tales from *Tasty-Fragrant* have been included in Leon Surmelian's *Apples of Immortalilty*.

26. Anne M. Avakian mentioned in *Armenian Folklore Bibliography*, xix, that she was able to locate only the second volume of the collection.

27. Stith Thompson's translation and enlargement of Antii Aarne, *Verzeichnis der Märchentypen* (*The Types of the Folktale: A Classification and Bibliography*), 2d ed. FF Communications 184 (Helsinki: Suomalainen Tiedeakatemia Academia Scientiarum Fennica, 1961). Tale type numbers used in this introduction are from this index.

28. V. P. Anikin, *Russkoe narodnoe poèticheskoe tvorchestvo: Uchebnoe posobie dlia filologicheskikh fakul'tetov pedagogicheskikh institutov*, ed. Nikolai Kravtsov (Moscow: Prosveshchenie, 1971), 103.

29. Leon Surmelian, *Apples of Immortality*, 22.

30. G. O. Karapetian, comp. and trans., *Armianskii fol'klor*, 8, note 18.

MAP OF ARMENIA

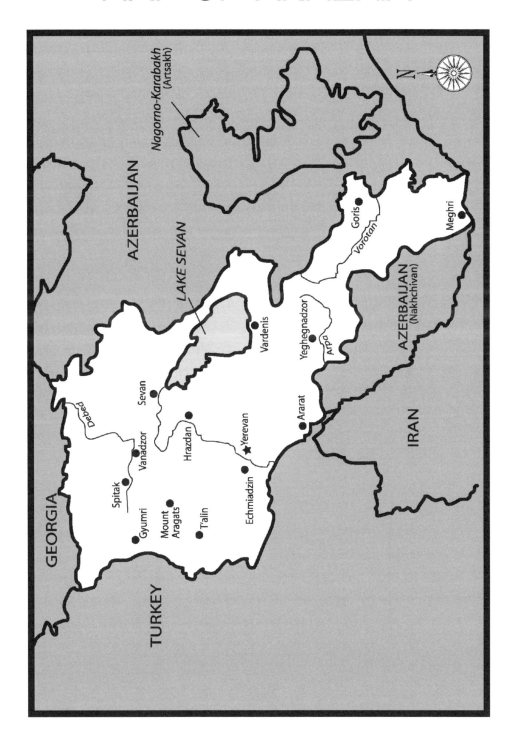

PART 1

ANIMAL TALES

THE TAILLESS FOX

Whether it happened or not, there once lived an old woman. One day she went to the barnyard to milk her goat. After milking the goat, she put the jug of milk on the ground and went to collect brushwood for kindling. She intended to start a fire with the kindling in order to boil the goat's milk.

A fox came along and poked her snout into the jug. The fox began lapping the milk. When she saw what the fox was doing, the old woman attacked the fox with a hoe and cut off the fox's tail.

The tailless fox ran away. The fox climbed onto a stone and begged, "Grandma, oh, grandma, give back my tail! I'll attach it and join my friends. After all, I don't want my friends to ask, 'Where did you disappear, tailless fox?'"

"If you want my help, bring me some milk in return for your tail," the old woman answered.

The fox went up to a cow and spoke in a pleasing manner. "Little cow, dear, dear, little cow, please give me some milk. If you do, I'll take the milk to the old woman, and in return she'll give back my tail. Then I'll attach my tail and join my friends. I don't want my friends to make fun of me and ask, 'Where did you disappear, tailless fox?'"

"I'll give you some milk if you bring me some grass," said the cow.

The fox went to the field and begged in a pleasing voice, "Field, darling little field, please give me some grass. I'll bring the grass to the cow, who will give me some milk in return. Then I'll bring the cow's milk to the old woman, who will give back my tail. I'll attach the tail and join my friends. I don't want my friends to make fun of me and ask, 'Where did you disappear, tailless fox?'"

"If you want some grass, you must bring me some water," replied the field.

The fox approached a spring and begged, "Little spring, dear little spring, please give me some water. I'll take the water to the field, and in return the field will give me some grass. I'll bring the grass to the cow, who will give me some milk. Then I'll take the milk to the old woman, who will give back my tail. I'll attach my tail and join my friends. After all, I don't want my friends to make fun of me and ask, 'Where did you disappear, tailless fox?'"

"I'll give you some water if you bring me a jug in which to put the water," said the spring.

So the fox went up to a girl and begged in her soft, flattering voice, "Girl, my dear little girl, please give me a jug. I'll bring the jug to the spring, which will give me some water. Then I'll take the water to the field and sprinkle it on the soil so that the field will give me some grass. I'll bring the grass to the cow, who will give me some milk. Then I'll take the milk to the old woman, who will give back my tail. I'll attach the tail and join my friends. After all, I don't want my friends to make fun of me and ask, 'Where did you disappear, tailless fox?'"

"I will give you a jug if you bring me some beads," replied the girl.

The fox went to a peddler and begged in her pleasing voice, "Oh, peddler, darling peddler, please give me some beads. I'll bring the beads to the girl, who in return will give me a jug. Then I'll take the jug to the spring, which will give me water. I'll take the water to the field and sprinkle it on the soil. In return the field will give me some grass. I'll take the grass to the cow, who will give me some milk. Then I'll take the milk to the old woman, who will give back my tail. I'll attach my tail and join my friends. After all, I don't want my friends to make fun of me and ask, 'Where did you disappear, tailless fox?'"

"I'll give you some beads if you bring me an egg," said the peddler.

The fox went to a hen and begged in her soothing, pleasing voice, "Hen, dear little hen, please give me an egg. I'll bring the egg to the peddler, who in return will give me some beads. Then I'll give the beads to the girl, who will give me a jug. I'll take the jug to the spring, which will give me some water. I'll take the water to the field and sprinkle it on the soil. Then the field will give me some grass, which I'll bring to the cow. The cow will give me some milk in return for the grass. I'll take the milk to the old woman, who will give back my tail. I'll attach my tail and join my friends. After all, I don't want my friends to make fun of me and ask, 'Where did you disappear, tailless fox?'"

"If you want an egg, go bring me some grain," said the hen.

The fox went to the farmer and begged in her very pleasing voice, "Farmer, dear farmer, please give me some grain. I'll take the grain to the hen, and in return, the hen will give me an egg. Then I'll take the egg to the peddler, who will give me some beads. I'll take the beads to the girl, who will give me a jug. Then I'll take the jug to the spring, which will give me some water. I'll take the water to the field and sprinkle it on the soil. The field will give me some grass, which I'll take to the cow. The cow will give me some milk. I'll take the milk to the old woman, who will give back my tail. Then I'll attach my tail and join my friends. After all, I don't want my friends to make fun of me and ask, 'Where did you disappear, tailless fox?'"

The farmer took pity on the fox and gave her a fistful of grain.

Overjoyed, the fox brought the grain to the hen. The hen gave the fox an egg, which the fox took to the peddler. In exchange, the peddler gave the fox some beads, which the fox took to the girl. In return, the girl gave the fox a jug. The fox ran with the jug to the spring, which gave the fox some water. The fox sprinkled the water on the field, and in return the field gave the fox some grass. The fox took the grass to the cow, who gave the fox some milk. Then the fox took the milk to the old woman, who gave back the fox's tail.

The fox attached her tail and ran after her friends, who never, ever asked, "Where did you disappear, tailless fox?"

THE SNAKE AND THE FISH

*T*he snake and the fish became friends. "Little sister," said the snake, "take me on your back, and let's ride around the sea."

"All right," the fish answered. "Sit on my back, and I'll give you a ride. Come with me and explore the sea."

The snake curled around the fish, and the fish glided over the waves. The two creatures had not swum out very far before the snake bit the fish on the back.

"Little sister, why are you biting me?" asked the fish.

"I bit you by accident," answered the snake.

They swam out a little farther, and again the snake bit the fish.

"Little sister, why are you biting me again?" asked the fish.

"The sun made me dizzy," answered the snake, "and I didn't know what I was doing."

They swam out even farther, and once again the snake bit the fish.

"Little sister, why do you keep biting me?" asked the fish.

"It is my habit to bite," the snake replied.

"You know, I have a habit, too," said the fish, and she dove to the bottom of the sea, as was her custom. When she did, the silly snake swallowed too much water and drowned. Never again did the snake have a chance to bite the fish.

THE AVENGING FROG

A peasant was carrying a load of hay on a cart. Suddenly, a little frog fell beneath the wheel of the cart and by some miracle remained alive.

The frog's relatives and friends came running from all directions and expressed their sympathy. The more daring among them threatened to take vengeance on the peasant.

"Don't worry about it," the victim said. "I have already paid the peasant back. I scratched the wheel of his cart good and proper."

THE INVINCIBLE ROOSTER

*T*here was and there wasn't a certain rooster who dug in the trash and found some gold coins. He flew up onto the cottage roof and began crying, "Cock-a-doodle-doo! I've found some money."

The king overheard him and ordered his nazirs, or officials, and his viziers, or ministers of state, to take the gold coins away from the rooster and bring them to him.

The nazirs and viziers did as they were instructed and brought the coins to the king.

The rooster cried, "Cock-a-doodle-doo! The king has misappropriated my wealth!"

The king gave the gold coins to his nazirs and viziers and said, "Take the gold coins back to the rooster. I'm not going to let that rascal shame me before the entire world."

The nazirs and viziers gave the gold coins back to the rooster.

The rooster flew up onto the cottage roof and cried, "Cock-a-doodle-doo! The king is afraid of me, so he gave back my money."

The king got angry and barked an order to his nazirs and viziers. "Go grab that rascal," he said. "Cut off his head and boil him. Then give him to me. I'll eat him for dinner and then I'll be rid of him."

The nazirs and viziers did as the king had ordered. They caught the rooster.

As the king's men were carrying the rooster to the king, the rooster cried, "Cock-a-doodle-doo! The king has invited me to dinner." The king's servants slaughtered the rooster and placed him in a large kettle with the intention of boiling him.

But the rooster couldn't be stopped. "Cock-a-doodle-doo!" he cried. "The king has ordered that a hot bath be prepared for me."

The rooster was cooked and placed before the king.

Again the rooster cried out. "Cock-a-doodle-doo! I'm sitting down to eat with the king."

Enraged, the king grabbed the rooster and swallowed him, bones and all.

The rooster, already in the king's throat, nevertheless cried out, "I'm going down a narrow street. Cock-a-doodle-doo!"

The king saw that still the rooster couldn't be silenced. He ordered his nazirs and viziers to draw their sabers and stand in readiness to chop the rooster to bits should he cry out again.

The nazirs and viziers drew their sabers. They stood, ready to attack, the nazirs on one side and the viziers on the other.

When the rooster reached the king's stomach, he cried, "Cock-a-doodle-doo! I used to live in the bright world, but I've fallen into a dark kingdom."

"Chop him to bits," ordered the king.

The nazirs and viziers began chopping at the king's belly and cut it open. The rooster jumped out and ran away.

The rooster flew onto the palace roof and cried, "Cock-a-doodle-doo!"

THE FOX WHO WAS DECEIVED

*T*here once lived an old woman and an old man. They had a dog and a rooster. The dog grew tired of guarding the yard, and the rooster grew tired of getting up early every morning to awaken the household.

"We have too much work to do," complained the dog and the rooster.

Finally, the dog and the rooster decided to run away from the old couple. They resolved to escape to the forest, where they planned to live without working.

One morning before the old couple got out of bed, the dog crept out the door and went into the yard, where the rooster joined her. The runaways walked through the gate and made a dash for the forest.

The forest pleased the pair no end, so the rooster began singing loudly.

A fox heard the rooster's loud voice. "Aha! Someone is cock-a-doodle-dooing here. That's nice. Now I'll have a wonderful meal," thought the fox.

She hurried to the tree on which the rooster was perched. The fox approached him and asked, "How did you happen to show up here in the forest?"

"We came here to build a home," the rooster replied.

"Let's measure a plot of land for the building site," the fox proposed.

"Our engineer is over there beneath the bush," answered the rooster. "Ask him and see what he says."

The fox thought that there was another rooster under the bush. "That's wonderful," he thought. "Now I'll have enough to eat for two meals."

The fox rushed toward the bush.

However, when the fox drew near, the dog jumped out and grabbed the fox by the throat. The discouraged fox turned and ran away. As she ran, she gave a backward glance and yelled, "You'll never build a house with an engineer like that!"

THE COUNCIL OF MICE

*T*he mice convened a council to discuss the matter of how to save themselves from cats.

"Let's find a bell and put it around the cat's neck. When the cat draws near, we will hear the sound of the bell, and we'll have time to hide," proposed one of the mice.

"That's a sensible suggestion," said another mouse.

"Finding a bell is no problem," said a third mouse, "but who is going to hang the bell on the cat's neck?"

There was a long silence. Since there were no volunteers, the matter ended and was never discussed again.

THE SPARROW

*T*here once lived a sparrow who had a splinter in his claw. He flew hither and thither from place to place until finally he spied an old woman. The old woman was gathering wood for her stove. She intended to kindle a fire to bake some nice, fresh bread.

"Oh, grandma, grandma," the sparrow called. "First take this splinter out of my claw and then continue your work. If only I could peck at some grain in peace, without pain, then I wouldn't die of hunger."

The old woman took pity on the sparrow and took the splinter out of the sparrow's claw. Then she returned to her task. She took the wood home and started a fire in the stove.

Meanwhile, the sparrow hopped about. Finally, the sparrow returned to the old woman and began demanding his splinter back.

"I threw your splinter into the oven," said the old woman.

"Give back my splinter," demanded the sparrow, "or I'll take away your bread."

What could the old woman do? There was no help for it. She had to give the sparrow the bread. The sparrow took it and flew away.

The sparrow flew on and met a shepherd who was dining on milk without any bread.

"Oh, shepherd, shepherd," called the sparrow, "why are you dining only on milk, without any bread? Here, take my bread. Crumple the bread and put it into your milk. Eat to your heart's content. I'll just peck at a few bread crumbs so that I won't die of hunger."

The shepherd accepted the generous offer happily. Meanwhile, the sparrow began hopping about. Finally, the sparrow returned to the shepherd and began demanding his bread back.

"But I've already eaten it," said the shepherd.

"Well, since that is the case, give me a lamb in exchange."

What could the shepherd do? He gave the sparrow the lamb, and the sparrow flew away.

The sparrow flew on until he met some people who were gathered to celebrate a wedding.

The sparrow noticed that there was no meat on the table. "Don't worry," said the sparrow. "Take my lamb. Slaughter it and prepare something tasty for the celebration. I'll just peck at a small piece of lamb so that I won't die of hunger."

The celebrants did as the sparrow so graciously proposed. After they had eaten, the sparrow hopped here and there. Then the sparrow returned and demanded that the people give back his lamb.

"But we've already eaten the lamb," said the people. How can we give it back to you?"

"Either return my lamb," shouted the sparrow, "or I'll take away your bride."

After uttering these words, the sparrow grabbed the bride and flew away.

The sparrow flew on until he saw an *ashug*, a wandering minstrel beloved by the people, walking down the road.

"*Ashug*, oh *ashug*," called the sparrow. "Take my bride. Meanwhile, I'll go peck at some grain so that I won't die of hunger."

Then the sparrow began hopping about here and there. Finally, the sparrow returned and demanded that the minstrel give back the bride.

"But the bride has gone home to her fiancé," said the *ashug*.

"Either give back the bride, or give me your *saz*," demanded the sparrow. A *saz* is a musical instrument used by minstrels to accompany their songs.

The *ashug* had to give the sparrow his *saz*. The sparrow threw the *saz* over his shoulder and flew away.

The sparrow searched for a comfortable little spot. He looked around and lighted on the branch of a tree. There the sparrow took the *saz* and began playing and singing.

He sang:

> Tweet-tweet! Chirp-cheep
>
> I swapped a splinter for bread,
>
> And for the bread I got a lamb, instead.
>
> I swapped the lamb for a bride,
>
> And the bride for a *saz*.
>
> Now I carry a *saz* by my side,
>
> And I sing songs ever so sweet,
>
> Tweet-tweet! Chirp-cheep!

THE WOLF AND THE LAMB

A young lamb once lived in a shed. A wicked wolf got into the shed and grabbed the little lamb.

The lamb fell down on its knees and said, "God has placed me in your power. Eat me up, but before doing so, please fulfill my last wish—play a song for me on your trumpet. My ancestors told me that wolves are great trumpet players."

The wolf was flattered. He squatted down and howled at the top of his lungs.

His song awakened the dogs. The dogs rushed at the wolf and bit him.

The wolf ran out of the shed and rushed to the top of the hill. He sat down and began weeping and beating himself. "I am worthy of that attack. Who on earth would ever claim that I was a trumpeter? I've always been a butcher and the son of a butcher."

TWO FOXES

*T*here once lived two foxes. One of them knew forty professions, and the other fox knew only two. The fox that knew only two professions said to the fox that knew forty professions, "Let's be friends and live together."

"What on earth for?" asked the fox that knew forty professions. "Has something happened that I have need of you? For the time being I'm just fine and can get along without you."

Having received such a brusque answer to his proposal, the fox that knew only two professions decided to spite the obstinate fox. One day while wandering around the forest, she noticed a trap in which lay a huge hunk of meat.

She ran to the stubborn fox and said, "I bagged a kill and ate myself sick, but there's still a great deal of meat left. Although you didn't want to be my friend, I'm not unforgiving. Come with me, and I'll show you the place where the meat is lying."

The fox that knew only two professions led the fox that knew forty professions to the trap. No sooner had the stubborn fox caught sight of the meat than she threw herself onto it and got caught in the trap. No matter how hard she tried to get out of it, her efforts were in vain. She began begging the fox that knew only two professions to help her get out of the trap.

The sly fox that knew only two professions said, "If a man comes, pretend to be dead. He'll hit you on the head several times and pull you by the tail. Then he'll take you out of the trap to carry you home.

"I'll lie on the path and pretend to be dead. The man will see me, and he'll want to take me home, too. As soon as he puts you down on the ground to pick me up, you rush off in one direction and I'll rush off in the opposite direction. In that manner, we'll free ourselves since he won't be able to follow both of us."

The man came as predicted. He hit the trapped fox on the head several times and pulled her tail to make certain that she was dead. Then he took her out of the trap and began walking down the forest path.

Suddenly, he noticed that another fox was lying on the path. He stopped. Then he placed the first fox on the ground. Just as he stretched his arm out to grab the second fox, both foxes jumped up and ran away.

Afterward, the fox that knew only two professions said to the fox that knew forty professions, "You didn't want to be my friend, but I saved your life."

Since that day, both foxes have been living together in harmony and friendship. They go to the forest to hunt together all the time.

PART 2

MYTHS AND LEGENDS

SNAKE CHILD OTSAMANUK AND AREVAMANUK,* WHO ANGERED THE SUN

*T*here once lived a king who had no children. One day while he was hunting in the mountains, he saw a snake basking in the sun and playing with her young.

The king sighed. "Even the snake has children, but I am childless. I have neither son, nor daughter. I don't even have a baby snake as a child."

When the king returned home he was told, "A son has been born to the queen. The boy has a human head and the body of a snake."

The king named his son Otsamanuk, which means "snake child." Snake Child Otsamanuk refused whatever was offered him for food and demanded human flesh instead. The king ordered that every day a young maiden be brought to the palace to be the young snake's dinner.

The time came for the family of a poor peasant to take its turn. The peasant had two daughters—his own and a stepdaughter. "We'll take your daughter to the palace and give her to the snake," the peasant told his wife.

But the stepmother wanted to take the man's daughter to the palace instead. She quarreled with her husband and raised a row. She began getting the man's daughter ready to take to Snake Child Otsamanuk. The maiden wept, the father wept, but nothing could be done. In the morning they had to set out for the palace.

That night they lay down to sleep. The maiden fell into a deep sleep and dreamed a strange dream. Someone, she didn't know who, appeared to her in the dream and said, "Don't be afraid. Take a pitcher of milk, a knife, and an ox-hide with you. Go up to Snake Child Otsamanuk and slit his snakeskin. Then wash him with milk, and you'll see what happens."

In the morning, the maiden said to the peasant, "Don't cry, Father. Whatever will be, will be. I just want to take a pitcher of milk, a knife, and an ox-hide with me."

The peasant prepared everything his daughter had asked for and, hanging his head, took her to Snake Child Otsamanuk.

The unfortunate maiden was led to one of the rooms of the king's palace. The king's servants locked the maiden in the room so that she couldn't get out. The little maiden looked around. The half-darkened hall seemed enormous because the walls were shrouded in gloom. Without wasting any time, she covered her head with the ox-hide, concealing the knife in her breast. The pitcher of milk was nearby on the floor.

Suddenly, a rustle was heard. Through a small space in a fold of the ox-hide, the maiden saw Otsamanuk slither up to the pitcher of milk and begin drinking. After having sipped a little milk, Otsamanuk stopped. His narrow throat didn't allow him to drink any more. Then Otsamanuk curled up into a ring, placed his head on his tail, and went to sleep.

As soon as the snake was asleep, the maiden threw off the ox-hide and with a quick movement slit open Otsamanuk's snakeskin. Then she took the pitcher of milk and washed the snake's body.

After the snake child's entire body had been washed with milk, Otsamanuk awoke and began thrashing in convulsions. He thrashed so violently that he knocked the maiden off her feet with a blow of his tail. Staggering, she fell, knocking out her front tooth in the process and losing consciousness.

When the maiden came to, she beheld a handsome youth bending over her. Glancing around, she saw the broken pitcher, the ox-hide, and the snakeskin.

"Yes, it's me—Otsamanuk," said the young man. "You saved my life. The spell that was cast on me is broken. Now I am human."

The king and queen's happiness knew no bounds. Without further thought, they arranged the marriage of the maiden and their son. The maiden agreed joyfully to marry Otsamanuk.

As was the custom, the bride's family—father, stepmother, and stepsister—were invited to the wedding feast. For seven days and seven nights the wedding was celebrated. On the eighth day a misfortune befell them—enemies attacked the kingdom. Otsamanuk gathered his army and set out to battle the enemy.

Meanwhile, the maiden's stepmother, burning with envy, decided to exchange her own daughter for the bride. She was aided by the chaotic state of affairs resulting from the panic that reigned in town and at court and by the fact that the girls looked very much alike.

After dressing her own daughter in a wedding gown, the evil stepmother left her in the palace. Then she secretly took the peasant's daughter, Otsamanuk's lawful wife, out of town and left her in a faraway forest.

The maiden wandered for a long time until she stumbled upon a forest hut. A couple lived there with their handsome son Arevamanuk, who had golden, curly hair. The name Arevamanuk means Child of the Sun. Arevamanuk was very proud that he had been born so handsome and strong. However, his vanity spoiled his character so that he became very arrogant and haughty.

Arevamanuk's family protected the poor maiden as if she were their own. Their son became friends with the young woman. Their friendship became affection; affection became passion; and passion became love. Soon the maiden became Arevamanuk's wife.

One day Arevamanuk was hunting in the forest. He saw a young man standing on the bank of the river. The young man stood there surrounded by flames, as if he were on fire.

"Who are you?" asked Arevamanuk.

"I am Arekag, the Sun's Ray," the stranger answered.

"What are you doing here? Do you want to set the forest on fire? Get out of here! Be off!" Arevamanuk said, and he raised his sword threateningly.

"So the Sun's Ray gives you no peace? Since that is the case, know this. The night that descends tonight will be eternal for you. You will be able to live only at night. And woe be to you if the Sun's Ray falls on you, for then you will die. So don't waste time. Build yourself a sanctuary," said Arekag. Then he flashed with fire and disappeared.

Fear gripped Arevamanuk. He hurried to build a hut. After he had built it, he dared not show his face in daylight.

Arevamanuk's wife went in search of her husband and found him in a desolate corner of the forest. Arevamanuk told her everything. He told her about the terrible curse that had been placed upon him. His wife remained with him in the hut, having decided not to abandon him in his misfortune. Soon a son was born to them.

"You must leave here and go back to civilization," said Arevamanuk. "Otherwise, our son will grow up wild and unsociable."

He wrote a letter and gave it to his wife. She took the child and went to the home of Arevamanuk's parents, where she handed them their son's letter. Arevamanuk had written, "I am sending my wife and son to you. I must be nowhere but in my hut during daylight, or I will die."

Arevamanuk's parents took in their daughter-in-law and grandson joyfully. One day they heard their daughter-in-law rocking the child to sleep in the darkness. "Sleep, sleep, little son, lullaby-lullaby," she crooned.

A male voice repeated, "Lullaby-lullaby."

The parents were amazed. Who could it be? They pestered their daughter-in-law with questions. In the end she confessed. "That is your son, who sails here at night. He wants to see his little son. But don't call him into the house. He always must be in his hut at dawn, or he'll be struck down dead."

The old folks waited for night to fall. They crept into the garden. They saw their daughter-in-law rocking her son in her arms. Suddenly, they heard someone calling her and quietly making his way through the trees. They looked, and it was their son. They grabbed him, kissed and hugged him, and began dragging him into the house.

"Don't touch me," begged Arevamanuk. "I can't go into the house. I can't stay with you, or I'll die."

His parents didn't believe him and continued to drag him into the house. They gave him food and drink and began conversing. Arevamanuk forgot about everything else.

With the first ray of the sun, he fell to the ground. His breathing stopped. Life barely flickered in him. His mother and father melted into tears. They tore their hair out, but nothing could be done.

The next night Arevamanuk's mother had a strange dream. She dreamed that someone, she didn't know who, appeared to her and said, "Arise quickly. Don iron shoes, take an iron staff, and go west. At the place where your shoes are full of holes and your iron staff breaks, you will find the means of bringing your son back to life."

Arevamanuk's mother got out of bed. She donned iron shoes. She took an iron staff and set out toward the west. She journeyed for a long time, more than a year, more than two years. She passed through a country of white people and through a country of black people. Then only birds flew around her and wild animals roamed the countryside. Eventually, even the birds and animals weren't around. Finally, Arevamanuk's mother came to the edge of the world.

At the edge of the world stood a beautiful palace made of blue marble. She went up to the palace, and it was there that her iron staff broke into pieces and her iron shoes were full of holes. She went through a blue arch and came to a luxurious garden. After walking through the garden, she came to another blue arch. She passed through twelve arches in all until she came to a blue bedroom, where a thousand stars were lying quietly sleeping. Arevamanuk's mother walked on.

She saw a golden ottoman, where Louise, Queen of the World and the mother of Arekag, the Sun's Ray, was sitting.

Louise noticed Arevamanuk's mother and said, "Why have you come to me, woman?"

"I came to beg you to return life to my son," answered Arevamanuk's mother, and she made a low bow.

"You raised a bad son," answered Queen Louise. "You spoiled him. He became mean, and he wanted to kill Arekag, my son."

Arevamanuk's mother lowered her head. She blushed with shame and said, "You are right, Queen Louise, but he has suffered greatly, and he has changed. Forgive him and return his life. You are a mother, and I am a mother. You must understand me."

"Let it be as you wish," sighed the kind Queen Louise. "Hide over there behind the pearl blanket. Soon night will fall and Arekag, the Sun's Ray, will come home. He will bathe in the pool. When he comes out of the pool, scoop some water up and wash your son with it. He will come back to life."

As soon as she had uttered these words, Arekag entered, glittering with fire. He plunged into the pool. After he got out, Arevamanuk's mother scooped up some water and set out for home with a full pitcher. She washed Arevamanuk with the sun's water, and he was resurrected. The curse was removed.

Meanwhile, news of this miracle flew about the entire country. Having returned from war, Otsamanuk, the snake child, heard about it. When he came to the palace, he immediately understood that his wife had been changed for another.

He set out for Arevamanuk's to ask advice of Arevamanuk's mother and to find out whether or not she could help him in his grief to find a means of searching for his wife, without whom he would have been a snake child to this very day.

Otsamanuk was received well. Arevamanuk's parents invited Otsamanuk to sit at the table, and they began regaling him. Otsamanuk told them everything that had happened. When he got to the part where the maiden who saved his life had stumbled and fallen, breaking her front tooth, the daughter-in-law smiled, and her golden tooth glistened.

Otsamanuk recognized his beloved wife. Everyone was at a loss and didn't know what to do.

Otsamanuk called Arevamanuk aside and said, "You aren't to blame, Arevamanuk, and I'm not to blame. It's simply that our lives have taken shape in this manner. Let's test our destiny. Let's give our wife salty shashlik (*khorovats*) to eat.** Each of us will hold up a glass of water. Whomever she asks for a drink will be her husband."

They mounted their horses and rode to the field. The maiden came out of the house with the child in her arms and called, "Arevamanuk!"

Arevamanuk hurried to bring her some water, but then she called, "Otsamanuk!"

Otsamanuk dismounted too. The woman stood between them and said, "Arevamanuk, here is your son. I am giving him to you to raise. I am going with Otsamanuk because I am his lawful wife."

She took Otsamanuk's glass of water, drank it down, and left with him.

Three apples fell from heaven—one for the storyteller, one for the audience, and one for the person who notes the tale well.

---

*Pronounced Ótzmanook and Arévamanook.

**Shashlik, and the Armenian equivalent *khorovats*, is skewered kebabs of meat.

THE FLOWER OF PARADISE

*L*ong ago a merchant lived in our country. He had a daughter who was so beautiful that everyone called her "Flower." She really was like a flower—tender and beautiful. Her father was very proud of her.

One day as the merchant was preparing to travel to distant lands on business, he asked his daughter, "Daughter, what would you like me to bring home for you?"

"Father, please bring me the Flower of Paradise."

"Very well, I'll get it for you," he replied.

The merchant traveled to distant lands and completed his business there. Then he began searching for the Flower of Paradise. He asked about it everywhere, but no one knew how to grow it or where to look for it. Finally, he met an old man who pointed out the way to the Flower of Paradise.

"But be careful," warned the old man. "The White Dev guards the flower."*

But do you think that could discourage the father's loving heart? No indeed. The merchant set out down the road the old man had pointed out. Whether he walked for a long or short time, only he knows. Finally, he came to the place where the Flower of Paradise grew. The merchant saw the flower, bent over, and picked it.

Suddenly, a violent storm arose. It grew dark, and a horrible monster stood before the merchant. The monster was manlike, but it wasn't a man. It was beastlike, but it wasn't a beast.

The monster began roaring madly. "Why did you pick my flower? Now you must die for your transgression."

"Now you must die" echoed from all directions. The poor merchant, half alive, bowed to the monster. "Spare me, oh mighty creature. My daughter asked me to bring home the flower."

"I will spare you," roared the monster, "only under one condition—you must give me your daughter in exchange for your life."

"Agreed," said the merchant.

"Since that is the case, I grant your life. Return home and remember this—when the mountain opposite the windows of your home turns white, it will be a sign that I am coming after your daughter."

Of course, the monster was none other than the White Dev. Meanwhile, the merchant returned home. His daughter ran to meet him, embraced him, placing her hands around his neck, and kissed him. The father embraced his daughter and handed her the Flower of Paradise. He decided not to tell her what had happened. He decided not to tell anyone his secret, and he became very depressed when he thought about the future. Days and nights flew by as he thought about what had happened. He became more and more gloomy and sad.

One morning when he awoke, the merchant noticed that the mountain located opposite the windows of his home was covered with white snow. The merchant broke into tears. People came running and began asking the reason for his tears. The merchant could no longer hide the fact that he had promised to give his daughter to the monster. He told them that the White Dev was coming after Flower.

"Don't cry, Father," said Flower. "I'll go with the White Dev. One can't escape one's fate."

Meanwhile, thunder resounded. The White Dev broke into the house roaring, "Where is Flower? Where is she? Give her to me."

The surrounding trees began trembling and became covered with ice because of the White Dev's roar and his cold breath.

What could Flower's parents do? Dressed in her best clothes and holding the Flower of Paradise in her hand, Flower went to meet the White Dev.

The monster laughed triumphantly. He grabbed the beautiful maiden and carried her away. Flapping his wings, the White Dev raised such a storm that his hissing and whistling swallowed the light. Everything froze and died wherever the White Dev flew.

The monster carried Flower to the deepest ravine on Mount Ararat.** It was an inaccessible, gloomy place, covered with ice. There stood the crystal castle of the White Dev, which he abandoned from time to time to wander the earth. Wherever the White Dev traveled, he attempted to destroy every living creature. Cold and terror followed in his footsteps all over the earth. The White Dev incarcerated Flower in his cold castle.

Several months passed. At the beginning of spring when the White Dev was not in the castle, Flower managed to run away. The monster returned. Noticing that the maiden wasn't where she should be, he flew into a rage. The White Dev gathered all his evil forces and set out in pursuit of Flower. Turning into a storm, whistling and hissing, he pursued Flower, like a giant dragon.

Meanwhile, the maiden had reached the foothills of Mount Aragats.*** She looked around and saw that the White Dev was overtaking her.

He was horrible and frightening. The poor maiden gave a piercing shriek, crying out for help. It was God's will that at that moment a magic door opened before her. Passing through it, the maiden went into the interior of the mountain. The door immediately closed behind her under the White Dev's very nose.

The Flower of Paradise

The monster's rage knew no bounds. He beat the summit of Mount Aragats with his wings and roared, "Where is Flower? Where is she? Give her to me."

We leave the White Dev there roaring while we follow Flower. We'll find out what happened to her after she passed through the magic door. After passing through the interior of Mount Aragats, Flower found herself beside a garden fence. The garden resembled paradise. From the thousands of discordant sounds that permeated the garden, this song took shape:

> In an emerald palace, in a golden coffin,
>
> Enchanted by dark powers,
>
> Lies our Arin in his bower,
>
> And the whole world is in mourning.
>
> He will lie there
>
> Until like a dove she appears.
>
> Full of new life and joy,
>
> She'll hug and kiss our boy.

Flower entered the garden, which was filled with rejoicing and happy songs:

> Here she comes, our princess!
>
> Over here, over here! Your beloved is here.
>
> Now he'll be resurrected from death so drear,
>
> Our brave, enchanted Arin.
>
> Now our glorious prince arises,
>
> Our mighty Prince Arin-Armanelin.
>
> His bright eyes smile at us radiantly.
>
> The world's flowers and trees so unhappily
>
> Enchanted by the White Dev
>
> Will waken from the monster's evil spell.
>
> Joyful life will be revived as well,
>
> As will fragrant, sunlit dells.

Flower walked across the garden and into the emerald palace. In the center of the palace there was a golden coffin, in which a handsome young prince lay. He was neither alive, nor dead. He was barely breathing. As soon as Flower saw him, her heart was filled with grief. She burst into tears. Then she bent over the prince and kissed him. Flower's teardrops fell onto the youth's face. Slowly the prince opened his eyes and arose. He was like a birch tree growing in paradise. You have probably already guessed who he was. Yes, it was Arin-Armanelin.

"Who are you, beautiful maiden?" asked Arin-Armanelin. "How did you get here?"

Flower told the prince everything about her imprisonment by the White Dev. She added the information that he was chasing her even at that moment. "I can hear his hellish roar," she said.

"He put a spell on me several months ago, sending down a dream of death," said Arin-Armanelin." He does so every year. I am here until someone comes and destroys the evil spell. You are one of those who has done so, Flower. Now I will go fight the White Dev."

After uttering these words, Arin took his fiery sword and left. The two powers merged in a battle to the death. They fought so that no one could distinguish between sky and earth.

The White Dev roared like a dark cloud. Arin-Armanelin struck right and left with his sword, and the earth shook. The battle ended with the defeat of the White Dev. Howling, hissing, and whistling, he crawled back to his gloomy abode, located on the bottom of the deep ravine on Mount Ararat. He shut himself up there in his crystal castle. Peace fell to the lot of his fair victor. Happy days came to the Valley of the Araks River.****

Arin-Armanelin married Flower. Nature spread a beautiful carpet of roses and other flowers at their feet. People and animals, birds and even choruses of ants sang merry songs and hymns to them. Above them in the heavens stretched a marvelous bright rainbow, and the fresh spring sun smiled down on the earth.

These events are repeated every year. Every year the White Dev manages to place a spell on Arin-Armanelin, and every year the spell loses its power when Flower comes to rescue him.

This drama accounts for the change of seasons. It is winter on Earth while Arin-Armanelin sleeps and the White Dev holds Flower captive. And it is spring on Earth when Flower's kiss awakens Arin-Armanelin.

---

*The *dev* is variously interpreted to be a monster, dragon, serpent, or giant. In Armenian mythology, *devs* are immortal spirits who inhabit old ruins. Some are good, such as Aralez, who licks the wounds of warriors fallen in battle. Others, such as the dragon Vishap, are evil.

**Known to Armenians as Masis and once located in Armenia, Mount Ararat is now part of eastern Turkey. It was thought that Noah's ark landed on Mount Ararat after the flood, and the mountain is closely linked to the Armenians' sense of identity.

***An extinct volcano in northwest Armenia about 25 miles (40 kilometers) from the capital Yerevan, Mount Aragats is the fourth highest mountain of the Armenian highlands.

****The Araks River flows through eastern Turkey to the Caspian Sea.

SEVEN STARS

*T*here once lived six brothers. The youngest of the six brothers was very handsome. One day the handsome brother went hunting. After several hours, he stopped to rest on the bank of a stream. Soon he fell asleep.

Meanwhile, a maiden came to the stream to fetch water. After filling her jug with water, she noticed the handsome youth lying there and fell in love with him. She continued to watch him as he slept.

When the youth awoke, he saw the beautiful maiden standing before him and fell in love with her at first sight. "Let's leave this place together. Let's get married and build a house," he proposed.

"Very well," replied the maiden, "but first I must carry this jug of water home."

Once at home the girl told her parents that she wanted to marry the youth she had met by the stream and that they wanted to go away immediately.

The parents understood very well that because the girl was in love she would not change her mind. Therefore, they took their daughter with them and moved to a distant land.

The moment the maiden left her native country, a deep sleep fell upon the young man. He remained asleep beside the bank of the stream.

Several years later, the maiden's family returned to their old home. One day they sent the young maiden to the stream to fetch water. She saw that her beloved had remained on the very spot where they had parted. She called him by name, and he awoke from his deep sleep.

But the young man was no longer human. He had turned into an angel. He flapped his wings to take flight, but he fell to the ground and hurt himself badly.

Realizing that her beloved had died, the maiden's heart broke and she died, too. The handsome young man and the maiden were buried together. Shortly thereafter they became stars and ascended to the heavens.

When the older brothers learned about the tragic fate of their youngest brother, they died of grief. All five of them became stars and ascended into the heavens, where they were united with their brother and his beautiful bride.

To this day they are living together in the sky. At night you have only to turn your head and lift your eyes. You will see all seven of them in the heavens.*

---

*There are two famous groups of seven stars. One group of seven stars forms the Big Dipper, which is part of Ursa Major, the Great Bear Constellation. The other is the Pleiades, a cluster of stars in the constellation Taurus. In Greek mythology the Pleiades are the seven daughters of Atlas and Pleione who were placed among the stars by Zeus.

THE SUN MAIDEN AREV AND
THE FIRE SPIRIT KRAG

When earth gave birth to the human race, darkness and cold reigned. Arev and Krag were children then. They were just learning to walk. They lived with a tribe in one of the caves on Mount Ararat.*

The grown men of the tribe hunted for a living, and on more than one occasion they became victims of wild beasts. The wild beasts had sharp eyes that were capable of seeing man in the darkness. Only the strong could catch wild game, and the strong ate almost all the game themselves. For that reason, the golden-haired maiden Arev and the curly-haired youth Krag rarely were treated to juicy meat. Their childhood passed in dreams of food.

One day an unimaginable din filled the cave. Someone proposed that from then on the members of the tribe hunt together. The strong hunters didn't like the suggestion. Nevertheless, after long, violent quarrels, the people chose a leader whose word was to be law.

From then on, the leader ate first so that his strength wouldn't weaken. The strong hunters ate after the leader so that they would always be strong. The women and children ate last. The leader saw to it that the hunters always brought their game to the cave. Anyone who broke the law was driven away and soon became the prisoner of neighboring tribes or fell victim to wild beasts.

Even though life in the darkness and cold was difficult, the tribe prospered and grew. When the maiden Arev and the young man Krag finally had the ability to lift stones that were as heavy as those that the adults lifted, they were allowed to hunt.

One day Arev and Krag went to the forest. The wind, blowing in their direction, whispered that a tiger was near.

"We won't be able to run from the tiger. Let's climb this tree," said Krag.

The young people climbed onto the branches with the agility of monkeys. Fresh human tracks led the beast to the tree. The tiger lifted his mustached snout and began roaring. Arev shuddered. She fell onto Krag's shoulder. The young man lay in wait, clutching a stone firmly. Suddenly, the burning gaze of the predator lit up its face. Krag jumped down. With a blow of the stone he killed the tiger. Krag let out a cry of victory. He glanced proudly at Arev.

---

30   **Part 2: Myths and Legends**

Amazed to see that Arev was glowing and surrounded by shimmering light, Krag fell onto the tiger's dead body. Krag was frightened, but he couldn't take his eyes off the maiden.

"What's going on?" he asked.

"I don't know. The tiger's intense, hot glance has burned your face. It is enveloped in a hot flame. Your bravery has made your face handsome, and it has pierced my breast and is burning my heart. My soul is glowing," said Arev. Hot tears of love, happiness, and pain, the first tears shed on earth, flowed from her eyes.

Suddenly, Arev's tears turned to bright stars and ascended into the black sky. One of Arev's tears fell onto Krag's chest. He felt a burning pain in his chest, but somehow the pain felt sweet. Krag kept looking at Arev.

Then Arev remembered their situation. "Let's go," she said. "Our leader is waiting for us."

Krag hoisted the tiger's body onto his shoulders with difficulty. But it required even greater effort to take his eyes off Arev. The maiden walked ahead, illuminating the forest path with the glow of passion. The forest was lit with her radiance.

They entered the cave and illuminated the dark, cold corners with their warm light. Krag took long in assuring the inhabitants of the cave that he and Arev were not evil forest or mountain spirits. People gathered around Arev and Krag distrustfully. They glanced warily at the shining maiden and at the young man with the fiery face. Horror hardened their timid hearts.

In the cave, darkness gave way to light, cold to warmth. People began to glance around their abode. For the first time they noticed that they were all very different. They were struck by the beauty of some and the ugliness of others.

The leader noticed that there were quite a few beautiful maidens in the cave. Then his gaze was arrested by the young, strong hunters. His old heart blackened with envy. A spiteful shudder ran across his face. Light began oppressing the leader worse than had the darkness.

The same burden lay on the shoulders of the old women who had few teeth and much gray hair. They were afraid that now they wouldn't be needed by anyone because of their looks. They rushed to the leader and said, "Listen to us unworthy ones. Give the order for Arev and Krag to be killed. Let the darkness return. The less people see, the happier they will be."

"Kill them! Kill them!" The cave shook with the sound of their voices.

The leader raised his hand. In an instant, it grew quiet. Power had made the leader lonely and cruel. Even so, because he was the leader, he had to think deeper, see further, and be harder than the others. "In the dark it's more difficult for us to search for edible roots, to fish, and to hunt," he said. "But we can't let Arev and Krag stay together. Together they give out too much light." Thus spoke the severe leader.

The people did as he advised. They threw Arev into the sky, where she became the Sun. They bound Krag and passed him from cave to cave to ignite the cave fires with his burning face.

Every morning the Sun Maiden Arev rises and searches for the Fire Spirit Krag until evening. Thousands of years have passed, but the Sun Maiden Arev has not lost hope of finding her beloved. To this day her heart burns with passion and her soul shines with love.

The Fire Spirit Krag suffers a similar fate as he keeps people warm. As long as the Sun Maiden Arev and the Fire Spirit Krag love one another, they are immortal. People who love as intensely as they, are immortal, too.

---

*Known to Armenians as Masis and once located in Armenia, Mount Ararat is now part of eastern Turkey. It was thought that Noah's ark landed on Mount Ararat after the flood, and the mountain is closely linked to the Armenians' sense of identity.

HOW GOD TAUGHT THE GREEDY PRIEST A LESSON

*T*here once lived a greedy priest who had an only daughter, whom he loved very much. Because of his love of gold, the priest put golden lattices on his windows instead of iron lattices. "Oh," he sighed. "If only my walls, too, were made of gold!"

He went to church and prayed to God. "Lord, I beseech you to fulfill my request. May the walls of my room become gold."

After three days had passed, a man came to see the priest. "Listen here, priest, God has heard your prayer. A small pot is standing behind the church doors. Go and take it. Then go to the spring and wash yourself. Rinse out the little pot, fill it with water, and bring it home. Whatever you pour water on and touch with your hands will turn to gold."

The priest did as he was instructed. He carried the water in the pot home, and sure enough, whatever he poured water on and then touched with his hands turned to gold. He drank some of the water. Then he went into the garden with his beloved daughter and poured all of the water out onto the flowers. Then he began touching flowers, stones, and trees with his hands. Everything turned to gold.

"Father, why did you do that? The flowers won't smell sweet anymore."

"Daughter, take this rose," answered the priest. Take it to the jeweler, and find out how much money he'll give you for it."

The girl took the rose to the jeweler and brought home a small bundle of money.

"See, daughter, how much money you've brought," said the priest.

His daughter was happy. The priest was so overjoyed that he even lost his appetite. He didn't put a morsel in his mouth all day long.

The next morning, the priest's daughter said, "Father, I'm hungry. I want to eat."

"I don't," the priest replied. "Eat something yourself, but I'm not hungry."

The priest went to the garden and once again didn't eat anything all day long. That evening he came home and went to bed.

The second morning he got up and said, "I'm hungry, daughter. Go to the market and buy some fish."

The priest's daughter brought some fish home and made dinner. She gave the fish to her father.

As soon as the priest put his hand on the fish, it turned to gold. Then he took his fork and touched another piece of fish. It, too, turned to gold because the priest had drunk water from the little pot so that now everything that touched his throat turned to gold.

"I'll die of hunger," said the priest. And he burst into tears.

When his daughter saw the priest crying, she rushed to embrace him. "Father, why are you crying?" she asked.

The priest wept all the more, and his daughter wept too. When the priest returned her embrace, his daughter turned to gold.

The priest sobbed. "I had only one daughter, and she has turned to gold," he said.

He went to the garden and walked around the garden for a long time. Then he returned to the house, sat down, and began looking out the window. He saw a beggar sitting and gnawing on a crust of bread. It seemed to be a sign.

"Lord," he prayed, "I need nothing in the world, except to rid myself of this unfortunate golden touch. I would be better off poor."

In the morning, he went to church and prayed. "Lord, give back my daughter, give back my crust of bread. I don't need any gold."

Another day passed. The priest could barely stand on his feet because of his hunger and thirst. Again he went to church, and again he prayed to God to take from him what he had conferred upon him.

The man who had appeared from nowhere to announce that God had given him the golden touch came again. "Take the pot, priest," he said, "and go to the spring again. Wash yourself, and rinse out the pot. Then fill it with water. Sprinkle the water on everything you touched with your hands and turned to gold. Everything will become as it was before."

The priest did as he was instructed. As soon as he sprinkled his daughter with water, she sneezed and asked, "Father, have I been asleep long?"

"For a long time, daughter, for a long time."

The priest sent his daughter to market and asked her to buy bread and all sorts of food for dinner. The priest sat at the table and ate with his former appetite.

After he had eaten his fill, he broke the golden lattices on his windows. He gave the gold from the lattices to the poor, and from that day on he was no longer greedy.

BLAZING A TRAIL

*T*he enemy was pillaging Armenia, one settlement after another. Smoke from the conflagration stretched sorrowfully to the sky. The cries of children were carried on the wind. The living, surrounded by corpses, were being driven into slavery. Several people threw themselves into the abyss to avoid being enslaved. Behind the Armenians was death, and in front of them was blood and tears.

Mesrop Mashtots' heart was wracked with grief. He rubbed his burning forehead with his palms. He could sleep peacefully neither today, nor tomorrow, not until he had found a way to help the defenseless.

Neither could Mesrop's friend Markoz sleep. "The grief of one village doesn't touch the inhabitants of another village. Only a few people rush to help us. Our people are callous," said Markoz with a sigh.

"They aren't callous," replied Mesrop. "It's just that our people are divided by mountains and faiths and dialects. We must unite them and inflame them with a common goal. But where is the path to unity? Where is it, Markoz?"

"What if we build a church in our village? People from the surrounding villages will come to it to pray. People will stop being unaffected by their neighbors' sorrows. They'll stop censoring the customs and traditions of one another. What do you say, Mesrop?"

"That's a good idea!" Mesrop rejoiced. "That's just what everyone needs." Excited, he rushed off into the mist.

At dawn he returned. "You have a good idea, Markoz, but one mustn't build a church on the plain. Whatever is easily accessible won't become holy. We'll build our church on the mountaintop. And we won't build a place just for praying. Let this be the first church to which people come not to shed tears but to draw wisdom from one another. We've had enough weeping."

"There's no path to the mountaintop," objected Markoz.

"That's true. But we can't build a church in the village, or the church will lose its power as a symbol. It won't serve as a shield of defense or a sword of support. It must be located in a high place. When they climb up, people leave the ordinary behind. They break away from their cares and are cleansed of the unnecessary. It will be easier for them to assimilate new ideas there. From the mountaintop people will see more than just one village. The petty will be forgotten when people get a revealing view of their native land. But not everyone will be able to conquer these cliffs, Markoz. Therefore, first we must construct a path to the summit."

"But the length of our lives is not sufficient to construct a path to the summit. Have you thought about that?"

"Yes, I've thought about it, Markoz. Others will finish it for us."

"Mesrop, the people need a church. I'm not going to wait. I'm going to begin building a church."

"First you must make a path to the church."

The friends parted, dissatisfied with one another. Markoz began building a church in his native village. Mesrop began building a road up the mountain. After the passage of several years, Mesrop had built as many steps as a child could master without getting out of breath.

Meanwhile, Markoz had built a church. He was praised in the village, but no one ever went to his church, except a few old women. Markoz waved his hand in dismay. "Ignorant people," he thought.

Year after year Mesrop went a little higher, slowly moving forward. His name was generously showered with ridicule and gibes.

Having decided to make his friend listen to reason, Markoz went to him. "Mesrop, you pass for being intelligent, but you've turned out to be a child. There aren't even roads between the villages, and yet you crawl up the mountain. People lived for centuries before us without undertaking such a project. Why are you freezing and going hungry and going without sleep? Don't be a laughing stock. Don't shame your father's name. While you're wasting your time building a senseless road up the mountain, your own house is collapsing."

Mesrop turned in anger. "Markoz, now you're no better than the princes who defend their own household, and only their own. Who are you—a member of a sect straying from the path? Or are you an *ashug*, a folksinger and poet, singing the people's praises, but not showing them the way in difficult times? You would do better to pray."

Time flew like a restive racehorse. People were born as others were swept away. Growing gray, Mesrop hurried, fearing that there wasn't enough time left to finish his road. As the peak of the mountain neared, Mesrop's strength diminished.

Finally, the happy day arrived. Gray-haired Mesrop looked back from the top of the mountain. Stone steps ran like years down to the villages and the people.

"My steps are several miles long. But now these miles can be traveled in an hour. My life in exchange for an hour. Is that so bad?"

For the first time in many years, Mesrop smiled, rejoicing that paths from the diverse villages flowed into the path to the mountaintop. From that day on, the unattainable mountain was accessible. People climbed to the top of the mountain. They built a church there. They named the church after Mesrop Mashtots, creator of the Armenian alphabet.

Holy Father Mesrop, we ask that you pray to God on our behalf.

The monk Mesrop Mashtots (ca. AD 363–440) created the thirty-six letters of the Armenian alphabet in AD 405. Prior to his invention, priests had taught in Greek and Assyrian. Greatly respected and revered by the Armenian people, Mesrop Mashtots created schools, where his alphabet was taught, throughout Armenia. The existence of an alphabet made it possible for Armenians to develop their culture and retain their identity. The story above is one of the legends about Mesrop Mashtots.

THE BLACKSMITH, THE CARPENTER, AND THE FARMER

When King Alexander's palace was being built, he bestowed more praise on the blacksmith than on the carpenter and the farmer.*

The carpenter and the farmer began to envy the blacksmith. The carpenter said that after all he built places in which people lived. The farmer claimed that after all he grew food, without which people could not live.

When King Alexander heard about their claims, being a wise ruler, he summoned other wise men to the palace to help decide which of the three men to honor.

This is the answer the wise men gave. "It is said that Adam was the first man to till the soil. But in order to till soil, one needs implements. That means that the trade of the blacksmith was established earliest. The blacksmith makes implements for himself, the carpenter, and the farmer. Therefore, the blacksmith should be held in highest regard. The carpenter should be held second in regard because the farmer needs both the blacksmith to make tools and the carpenter to build him a house before he can begin to farm."

Then King Alexander and his wise councilors spoke to the carpenter and the farmer and convinced them not to be envious of the blacksmith.

---

* There is no indication whether this legend is about Alexander the Great (356–323 BC) or King Alexander (34–31 BC), son of Cleopatra and Mark Anthony, who ruled during the Artashesian-Artaxiad Dynasty of Armenia.

THE LEGEND ABOUT TIRIDATES (TRDAT) III

*T*he Armenian King Khosrov [AD 198–252] fought the Persians for ten years and so vexed the Persian king that he turned to his councilors and said, "I swear that I'll appoint as co-ruler whoever rids me of Khosrov."

The sly Anak volunteered to do just that. He appeared in Armenia with his possessions, wives, and children. He threw himself at Khosrov's feet and said, "Have mercy on me, my king. Give me shelter and protection from the Persians."

Warm-hearted King Khosrov did more than give him land on which to settle. Khosrov favored Anak and elevated him to the upper ranks. Anak waited for the opportunity and ran Khosrov through with a sword.

The dying king ordered his servants to pursue Anak and to destroy the traitor's family. Khosrov's servants overtook Anak at a river and drowned him. It was only by a miracle that Anak's son Gregory was saved.

Meanwhile, taking advantage of the murder of King Khosrov, the Persian king invaded Armenia and subjugated the country. Seeking to escape, Tiridates (Trdat) III,* the son of the Armenian king, had to flee to Rome. He lived there for a long time, learning the military arts.

When the Goths attacked Rome, the outcome of the impending battle was to be decided in a single combat. The Roman Caesar had to fight the leader of the Goths. Not wanting to risk harm himself, the Roman Caesar started searching for a substitute among his warriors.

"Allow me to take your place, Caesar," volunteered Tiridates. Arrayed in royal armor, Tiridates advanced fearlessly on the enemy.

So great was his strength that he lifted the Goth with his mighty arms and threw him to the feet of his sovereign. The Goths, impressed by the mighty warrior, retreated.

As he was celebrating the victory, Caesar gave Tiridates the following promise. "I will give you legions so that you can return your father's throne to its rightful heir. You shall rule Armenia!"

When Tiridates obtained his father's kingdom, he decided that it was the Roman gods who had helped him. He ordered that a sacrifice be made to them. The happy servants of Tiridates rushed to fulfill his command. His officials and household members merrily made preparations to participate in the triumphant ceremony.

Only Tiridates' faithful friend and advisor, Gregory, frowned and looked askance. Gregory was the son of Anak. Long ago he had managed to make amends for his father's sin through his devotion to Tiridates.

"Why aren't you taking part in our celebration, my friend?" Tiridates asked Gregory.

"Because I can't bow down to idols, Sovereign. There is no God on earth, except Christ."

This unexpected confession seemed to Tiridates to be an unprecedented betrayal. "So, you are a Christian!" He gasped with anger and ordered that Gregory be hanged upside down and that his mouth be gagged so that no one could hear him speaking.

Gregory hung upside down for seven days and praised Christ the entire time.

"Is he still alive?" asked the astonished king, who tried to break the will and faith of his former friend. "You call on your God in vain because you won't receive any help from him."

Tiridates dreamed up new tortures for Gregory. He beat the holy man with sticks and poisoned him with smoke, and stuck sulfur mixed with salt and vinegar into his nostrils. He pounded nails into the soles of his feet and made him walk. He dragged Gregory, with nails stuck all over his body, along the ground.

Rage clouded Tiridates' reason, not allowing him to stop. Finally, in order to be completely rid of Gregory, Tiridates ordered that he be thrown into a deep pit that was full of snakes.

But the snakes didn't touch the saint. There was a widow who wouldn't let Gregory die of hunger. Every day she came to the pit and brought him a meager meal.

At that time the Roman Emperor Diocletian [AD 284–305] sent couriers to all parts of his empire in search of a wife. The Christian Hripsimé, who had taken a vow of celibacy, was reputed to be the most beautiful of all women. She and her sister nuns spent all their time in prayers and conversations with the Mother Superior Gayané. A portrait of Hripsimé was made and was sent to Diocletian.

Struck by the maiden's beauty, the Emperor immediately sent her a letter with a proposal of marriage. How could Hripsimé break her vows and marry a pagan? Hripsimé made secret preparations to run across the border to Armenia with the Mother Superior Gayané and the other nuns.

After learning about their flight, Diocletian appealed to Tiridates with a request. "The Christians lured away Hripsimé, and she has fled to Armenia. Find her and send her to us. If you wish, marry her yourself."

A search was announced, and the runaway was found. Hripsimé really was a heavenly beauty. Tiridates ordered his servants to clothe her in royal dress and deliver her to the palace. The guards had scarcely set out to fulfill the king's order when a terrible deafening clap of thunder resounded. The frightened soldiers ran to Tiridates at full speed to tell him about the miraculous sign.

"Pathetic cowards, you're afraid of thunder!" he screamed at them. Then he sent an entire legion after Hripsimé with the order to kill all of her companions.

Hripsimé came out to meet them herself. "Don't touch anyone, and I'll go to the king."

When he saw Hripsimé, Tiridates immediately was captivated by her and wanted to embrace her. As soon as he approached her, she avoided his caresses.

The king left the room and sent for Gayané, the Mother Superior. "Have the old woman convince the girl to submit to me, or else a cruel death awaits all of them," commanded Tiridates.

Gayané entered. When they let Gayané see Hripsimé, she began persuading Hripsimé not to fear the king's threats. Tiridates was informed of Gayané's perfidy. They seized the Mother Superior, broke her teeth with stones, and drove her from the palace.

The king approached Hripsimé again, but as before he couldn't get control of her. Then he was seized with rage.

The next morning all of the maidens were subjected to terrible torture. They were burned with candles and hacked to pieces. Gayané, the Mother Superior, was the last to die and suffered especially cruel torture.

A week went by. The king set out on a hunting expedition as if nothing had occurred. Then something happened to him and his companions. A strange, unprecedented illness struck them. They began snarling at one another. They attacked people and bit them. Nothing seemed to help them.**

At that time Tiridates' sister had a dream. A splendid, awe-inspiring young man appeared to her and said, "Tiridates will be healed if Gregory is taken out of the pit."

Upon awaking, the princess wondered about the dream. "Fourteen years have passed since Gregory was thrown into the pit. Could he still be alive?"

In any event, she sent a servant to Gregory. "Are you alive, Gregory?" the servant called to the saint in the pit.

"I am alive," Gregory answered.

Pale, thin, and covered with tangled hair, Gregory appeared in the light of day. Filled with shame, the servants led him to Tiridates, who was roaring like a wild boar in his insanity.

But Gregory didn't want to heal Tiridates right away. First he gathered the remains of the innocent maidens and grieved over the torments of Christ's brides and the evil insanity of their torturers. Then he ordered that a church be erected, and he brought their remains to that place.***

Gregory brought Tiridates to the bodies of the slain maidens. Tiridates was obedient to the will of the saint and begged pardon for his great sin. Tiridates prayed for the protection of the holy maidens.

Tiridates' remorse was so sincere and his prayers were so fervent that he was healed. After he was healed, he received grace. After he received grace, he had faith. After he had faith, he received blessedness. And after blessedness, he received holiness. Gregory baptized Tiridates, and Tiridates made Christianity Armenia's state religion.

Then Tiridates built churches and established monasteries. At the same time he became so meek that it was with difficulty that people recognized their former torturer and tyrant. It is said that toward the end of his life, he was like a hermit and that he attained an unusual spiritual eminence.

After receiving the rank of bishop, Gregory the Illuminator never stopped preaching the gospel. He preached not only to the Armenians, but he enlightened other people as well. He established many Christian cloisters. At the end of his life, he went out into the wilderness to spend his remaining days in contemplation.

Saints Gregory, Hripsimé, Gayané, blessed maidens, and King Tiridates, pray to God for us.

---

*Tiridates (Tiradáytes) is the English name, and Trdat (Trdát) is the Armenian name, of Khosrov's son.

**Tiridates (Trdat) III was struck with lycanthropy as punishment for his sinful cruelty.

***Churches (the Church of Hripsimé in AD 618 and the Church of St. Gayané in AD 630) were built near Armenia's mother cathedral, Echmiadzin Cathedral, in honor of the martyred nuns. Hripsimé and Gayané were sainted.

THE MIRROR

*A*fter conquering many countries, Tamerlane (Timur Leng) went to Europe. In Europe he saw a mirror for the first time. When he saw his ugly face reflected in the mirror, he burst into tears. He wept all day long.

The next morning he noticed that his vizier, or advisor, was crying. Timur asked his vizier why he was crying. The vizier answered nothing, but continued to cry all week long.

Timur asked his vizier again, "Listen here, why have you been crying for such a long time. What has happened?"

"Why wouldn't I cry?" asked the vizier. "You saw your face in the mirror just once and you burst into tears. But I see your face every day."

The Mongol Tamerlane (1336–1405) invaded Armenia in 1386–1387, 1394–1396, and 1399–1403. He declared that he was the descendent of Genghis Khan, and he established a vast empire that stretched from the Black Sea to India. He was named Timur Leng* (Timur the Lame) because his left side was partially paralyzed. Tamerlane (Timur Leng) was famed for his cruelty and paradoxically for his support of the arts and education. The Armenians, like the other peoples conquered by Timur, harbored no fondness for him. In the tale above, the ugliness of Timur's behavior is reflected on the physical plane.

---

*Some sources render the spelling Timur Leng, and others render the name as Timur Lenk.

WHY THE ONION IS BITTER

*I*n the old days the sweet Onion and the bitter Watermelon were neighbors. In those times, the Onion was the size the Watermelon is now, and the Watermelon was the size the Onion is now. The Onion had not a care in the world. It grew stout and heavy. Only one thing was wrong—the Onion was bored.

One day the Onion heard a rustling beyond the garden. The Onion knew that it had nothing to be afraid of, but having nothing to do, it began listening. The rustling developed into a frequent breathing. The Onion wanted to see who was there, but it was too lazy to look. Finally, it couldn't bear it any longer and turned its bulky, corpulent body around.

Beyond the garden the sickly Plantain, covered with sweat, was struggling to make its way through a clump of grass.

The Onion was well watered, so no matter how hard it tried, it couldn't keep still. "Listen, barebelly," the Onion said to the Watermelon. "Do you hear the Plantain panting again?"

"It's hard for the poor fellow," the thin Watermelon answered.

"What 'poor fellow'? The Plantain is just a smart aleck," the Onion fumed. "They barely throw it out of the garden when it grabs onto a clump of grass."

"It's not easy for the Plantain," sighed the Watermelon.

"You harp on the same theme—'it's not easy, not easy,'" fumed the Onion. The Onion regretted striking up a conversation with the Watermelon. It grew silent. But boredom always tires the well-fed, so the Onion condescended to converse with the Plantain.

"How did you know how to struggle out of the clump of grass, Plantain?"

"I am satisfied with little and work very hard," the Plantain whispered barely perceptibly, for it was still covered with earth up to its shoulders.

"The farmer cuts you out here, and you grow over there. He tears you up by the roots, and you appear alongside the garden. Where do you get such strength of spirit that you don't perish in endless persecutions?"

"Strength of spirit is hardened in battle," answered the Plantain slightly louder while freeing its chest from the clod of earth pressing on it.

"In battle, you say? What makes you strong?"

"My enemies make me strong," the Plantain answered resoundingly.

The Onion couldn't bear high tones, and the Plantain's voice grated him. Satiety needs contemplation and peace, rather than loud noises. Therefore, the Onion frowned and asked with a grin, "Tell me, Plantain, what is the most difficult thing to do—to die of thirst in the sun, to be crushed by a horse's hoof, to be torn up by the roots, or to be chopped to bits by an unrelenting Spade?"

"The most difficult thing to do is to avoid offending another creature."

The Onion raised itself slightly and exclaimed in amazement. The Plantain had already raised children.

The Onion was frightened. "The Plantain has raised children. They'll drink all the water that people pour on me. Then I'll have to obtain water myself out of the hard, stingy, gloomy depths of the soil. No, no, not that!"

The horrified Onion began shouting, "Spade, come here quick!"

The Watermelon tried in vain to stop the Onion, who cried out all the louder.

Finally, the Spade appeared and began carelessly chopping up the rebel. The Plantain was chopped up just for being alive and living on its own patch of earth.

"Oh, Onion," cried the dying Plantain, "idleness and laziness have given rise to envy and have led you to treachery. If there is justice on earth, may you become as bitter as is my fate. Watermelon, for your kindness may you become as full as my hopes and as sweet as my dreams."

The fierce Spade was sharp, sharp but blind. The Spade felt that it had destroyed the Plantain, but it didn't see that it was sowing the Plantain's children. They were washed with the moisture of the Plantain's tears and with the juice of the Plantain's body.

Beside the Plantain's grave, the Plantain's children soon began struggling to emerge into the light. It was easier for them in the loosened, moist earth, and they grew quickly.

The Onion saw them, and bitterness burned it. The Onion began to dry up. The Onion ate itself up with helpless rage and began growing smaller before its very eyes.

When the Watermelon saw the Plantain's children, the sweetness of happiness flowed through its soul. When the Plantain's grandchildren made their appearance, the Onion looked like it looks now and the Watermelon looked fat and full, as it is today.

PART 3

FAIRY TALES

LITTLE BEAR

*T*here once lived a priest. He was so strong that every day he hoisted the church up onto his back and carried it to the forest. After saying his prayers there, he hoisted the church up onto his back once again and returned it to its original place.

One day after he had hoisted the church up onto his back and was carrying it to the forest, he met a bear-cub by the name of Little Bear.

"Why are you carrying the church to the forest?" Little Bear asked.

"To pray," the priest answered.

"You don't say!" exclaimed the bear. "If you are so strong, let's fight. Whoever wins will eat the loser."

"All right then," said the priest. "Let's fight!"

They grappled, and the bear-cub lifted up the priest. He banged the priest down on the ground and wanted to rip him to pieces, but the priest begged, "For the love of God, please don't kill me, and I will take you home and take care of you."

Little Bear agreed to the priest's proposal and went with him to his village. Once there, Little Bear gobbled down all the priest's supplies, and the poor priest didn't know how to get rid of the beast. Finally, he decided to give Little Bear to the king as a gift to get him off his hands. It was no sooner thought than done. The priest led Little Bear to the king.

The king accepted Little Bear as a gift and found him to be most amusing. One day passed, and a second day passed. The king saw that soon Little Bear would destroy his entire kingdom. No matter how much the king fed the bear-cub, the bear said, "I'm hungry!"

"I'll have to send the bear-cub somewhere far away," thought the king.

The king ordered his nazirs, or officials, and viziers, or ministers of state, to summon a sorceress. They brought an old woman to the king. The king asked if she knew of a place the bear-cub could be taken, from which he could never return.

"Of course, I know of such a place, my Lord. Send him into the forest to fetch wood. Send him to the forest that is beyond seven mountains, where the forty *devs* live.* They are brothers, and they will tear your bear-cub to pieces so that only his ear will remain in one piece."

"That sounds good," the king rejoiced.

He summoned Little Bear and said, "Go to the forest beyond the seven mountains and bring back a hundred cartloads of wood."

"Your wish will be fulfilled. Give me a hundred carts and a hundred carters, as well as supplies for the road. Obtaining the wood will be my business."

Little Bear got everything that he wanted from the king and set out. Singing songs, Little Bear rode behind the carts. When dusk overtook him, he stopped. He slaughtered one of the draught oxen, cooked it, and dined with the carters. After dining, he harnessed the oxenless cart to the others and went on his way. In that manner, they reached the edge of the forest beyond the seven mountains. Finally, Little Bear slaughtered the last ox, cooked it, and sat down to dine.

The *devs* saw a column of smoke rising over the forest, and they were amazed. Who would dare come near? Neither a bird on the wing nor a snake crawling on its belly would be so bold as to force its way through to this part of the world. The eldest *dev* sent the youngest to find out what the smoke was.

The youngest *dev* saw Little Bear and a hundred men around a campfire. "Who are you?" he shouted. "Why have you come, and why have you made a campfire on the edge of the forest? Are you spirits, people, or beasts? Answer! No one can escape the *dev* brothers."

Little Bear was furious. "Come a little closer and let's see who you are and why you are bragging. Come here, and you'll find out who we are."

As soon as the *dev* approached, Little Bear hit him with a club. The *dev* collapsed. Little Bear tied him to the cart so that he wouldn't escape and sat down to his meal again.

When the eldest *dev* noticed that his brother had not returned, he sent another brother to fetch him. Little Bear made short work of him, too, and tied him to the cart beside his younger brother. In this manner, Little Bear tied up thirty-nine *devs*.

The eldest *dev* awaited his brothers, but they did not return. Enraged, he decided to go himself.

When he arrived, he saw all thirty-nine brothers bound and lying side by side. Little Bear was sitting by the campfire dining with a hundred men.

"What kind of people are you, and what are you doing here?" asked the eldest *dev*.

Without uttering a word, Little Bear hit the *dev* with his club and tied him up, too.

At dawn Little Bear ordered the forty *devs* to chop down trees in the forest and to load them onto the carts. The *devs* rushed to the forest, and in an hour they had chopped so much wood that there was enough to fill a hundred carts, and then some.

Little Bear tied the hundred carts together and harnessed the *devs* to the carts. He sat atop the load of wood and drove the *devs* on with a whip. The *devs* traversed the six-month distance in a month.

It was announced to the king that Little Bear had come back. The king was at a loss. He ordered that the head of the old woman sorceress be chopped off immediately because he considered that the sorceress had deceived him.

Little Bear unloaded the carts in front of the king's palace. He sent the *devs* home and went to the king to inform him that he had brought the wood. The king pretended to be happy, but in his soul of souls it was as if cats were scratching him.

The king summoned another sorceress and asked whether she knew a place he could send Little Bear, from which he would never return.

The sorceress said, "The King of Frangistan** has a beautiful daughter. Order Little Bear to bring her to you. Whoever travels to the land where she lives never returns."

The king obeyed the old woman. He summoned Little Bear and ordered him to travel to Frangistan and bring back the king's daughter to be his wife.

"Very well," Little Bear said. "You may be assured, my Lord, that I will fulfill your wish."

As soon as dawn came, Little Bear set out for Frangistan. Only God knows whether he traveled a long or short time. Suddenly, he came upon a man chasing a hare. The Runner caught the hare, even though he had a millstone tied to each foot.

The Runner noticed Little Bear and asked, "Where are you going, Brother Bear?"

"I'm going to Frangistan on behalf of my king, who is seeking the hand of the daughter of the King of Frangistan in marriage."

"Take me with you."

"All right. Let's go. There'll be two of us. The more the merrier."

The pair traveled on until they came to a man standing in the middle of the sea, drinking seawater. He was sucking up huge quantities of seawater and saying, "Oh, I'm dying of thirst."

The Drinker noticed Little Bear and the Runner and asked, "Where are you going? Won't you take me with you?"

"All right. Let's go. There'll be three of us. The more the merrier."

Little Bear, the Runner, and the Drinker traveled on. Whether they traveled a long or short time, only God knows. After a difficult journey, they reached a mill that had seven millstones. They entered the mill and saw a miller grinding grain into flour. The Miller wasn't waiting for the flour to be kneaded into dough and baked into bread. He was swallowing raw flour and howling, "Oh, help me, I'm dying of hunger!"

"Hello, Brother Miller," said the travelers.

"Hello, where are you headed?"

"We're going to Frangistan to fetch the king's daughter and bring her to Little Bear's king," said the Drinker.

"Won't you take me with you?"

"All right. Let's go. There will be four of us. The more the merrier."

The four companions traveled on. Whether they traveled a long or short time, only God knows. Finally, they came upon a man who had placed his ear to the ground and was listening. The Listener was talking to himself.

"Hello, Brother Sage," the travelers said.

"May your children be healthy, and may God help them. Where are you going?"

"We're going to Frangistan to fetch the king's daughter and bring her to Little Bear's king," said the Drinker.

"May I join you?"

"Why not? Let's go. There'll be five of us. The more the merrier."

The group traveled on and came to a man playing the *saz*, which is a stringed instrument. As he played, mountains, dales, and stones—all of nature—were dancing. Even the heavenly birds were flying and dashing here and there as they listened to the *saz*.

"Hello, Brother *Ashug*,"*** they greeted him.

"Hello, where are you going?"

"We're going to Frangistan to fetch the king's daughter and bring her to Little Bear's king," said the Miller.

"Please take me with you."

"Why not? Let's go. There'll be six of us. The more the merrier."

The six companions traveled on until they came to a man who had hoisted Mount Ararat**** onto his back and was shifting it from side to side.

"Hello, Brother Strong Man. What are you doing?" asked the travelers.

"I'm testing my strength. And where are you going?"

"We're going to Frangistan," said the travelers.

"May I join you?"

"All right. Let's go. There'll be seven of us. The more the merrier."

They traveled on—Little Bear, the Runner, the insatiable Miller, the Drinker, the Sage, the *Ashug*, and the Strong Man. Finally, they reached Frangistan, where they knocked at the king's gate. A servant came and asked them what they wanted.

"We want to speak to the king," said Little Bear.

The servant went to the king and informed him that Little Bear and several strangers wanted to speak to him.

"Let them come in. Let's see what kind of people they are," said the king.

The servant summoned the group. Little Bear and his companions entered and stood before the King of Frangistan.

"Hello, Your Majesty," Little Bear said. "We came to fetch your daughter for my king, who wants to marry her. If you give her willingly, everything will be fine. But if you don't give her to us, we'll take her by force."

"I'll give her to you," said the King of Frangistan, "but first you must fulfill my three wishes. If you fulfill my three wishes, my daughter will be yours. If you don't fulfill my wishes, it will be off with your heads!"

"Agreed," Little Bear said. "We'll fulfill your wishes. If we fail, you may do whatever you want with us."

The king's first wish was that the travelers eat everything placed before them. He issued a command throughout the entire kingdom for each home to bring a big pot of soup for his guests. And he ordered his cooks to bake bread all day long and deliver it to the palace.

It was no sooner said than done. Each family brought a big pot of soup. There was so much soup that it would feed a thousand people and still there would be some left over. The king's guests ate everything and still wanted more.

The King of Frangistan was amazed. "It didn't work out as I had thought," he said. "I'll have to think up a more difficult task, or else these monsters will ruin my daughter."

He summoned Little Bear and said, "Beyond seven mountains, there is a spring that contains the water of life. I'll send my man after the water, and you send yours. The man who returns first will win."

Little Bear agreed. He called the Runner and ordered him to bring back the water of life from beyond the seven mountains.

"Your wish will be fulfilled, Brother Bear," said the Runner. "There could be nothing easier."

It must be confessed that a week beforehand the king had sent a horseman on a racing horse after the water of life. The distance was far. It would take more than two or three weeks for a good rider to go there and back. But the Runner caught up to the king's horseman, passed him, scooped up the water of life, and brought it back.

The king's messenger had barely reached the spring when the Runner was already back at the palace. The Runner gave the water of life to the King of Frangistan.

"There's no disputing that your man won," said the king. "I have one last wish. If you fulfill it, there's no help for it—my daughter will be yours. I've ordered that a bath be heated for you. Go and wash up. Then come dine with us. After dinner, you may take my daughter away."

Little Bear and his companions went to the king's bathhouse. Meanwhile, the king had ordered his servants to heat the bath so hot that his guests would be burned alive.

Little Bear saw that the fire blazed so that the walls of the bathhouse were red. He sent for the Drinker and asked him to cool the bathhouse down. The Drinker spewed a stream of cold water from his mouth and cooled the walls and the water in the bathhouse.

The seven companions entered the bathhouse, washed up, dressed, and went to the palace to dine.

The King of Frangistan understood that he had not succeeded in tricking Little Bear. Therefore, he ordered the servants to sprinkle poison in the dishes in order to poison his guests. Otherwise, there would be no escaping these bold fellows.

The Sage had placed his ear to the ground and had heard that the dishes were to be poisoned. He whispered to the others and warned them not to eat anything.

When the *Ashug* learned about the plot, he began playing his *saz*. The king, his wife, his daughter, and the servants listened spellbound. While they were listening captivated, the companions grabbed the bowls of poisoned food and sprang into action. They passed the bowls of poisoned food to the king and the members of his household. They transferred the king's bowls to the seven friends. The *Ashug* put down his *saz*, and everyone began dining.

The King of Frangistan ate from the bowl and immediately fell off his chair. His wife died of fright.

Now Little Bear's time had come to take the King of Frangistan's daughter to his king. After a moment's reflection, Little Bear changed his mind and decided to marry the King of Frangistan's daughter himself. After all, his king had not treated him very well. Why return to him?

Little Bear and his friends went to war against the king with whom he had lived before. Little Bear vanquished him and ascended the throne himself. He married the daughter of the King of Frangistan. The wedding was celebrated for seven days and seven nights, and everyone lived happily ever after.

Three apples fell from heaven—one for the storyteller, the second for the person who asked for the story to be told, and the third for the person who listened to the story.

---

*The *dev* is variously interpreted to be a monster, dragon, serpent, or giant. In Armenian mythology, *devs* are immortal spirits who inhabit ruins. Some are good, such as Aralez, who licks the wounds of warriors fallen in battle. Others, such as the dragon Vishap, are evil.

**Frangistan (sometimes spelled Frankistan or Farengstan) is Western Europe.

***Folksingers and poets are called *ashug*s in Armenia.

****Known to Armenians as Masis and once located in Armenia, Mount Ararat is now part of eastern Turkey. It was thought that Noah's ark landed on Mount Ararat after the flood, and the mountain is closely linked to the Armenians' sense of identity.

OKHIK

*T*here once lived a man and his wife. They had just one son. One day the father took his son with him to find a master craftsman to whom he might apprentice the boy.

Having reached a spring, the peasant stopped. He quenched his thirst and sighed, "Oh, how nice!"

Okhik, who lived at the bottom of the spring, heard the father say "oh" and thought his name was being called. He came to the water's surface and standing before father and son asked, "What do you want of me? Where are you going?"

"I am seeking a master craftsman to whom I might apprentice my son," answered the father.

"Give me your son. I am a master craftsman," said Okhik.

The father gave Okhik his son. Okhik grabbed the boy and dove down deep into the water. The father returned home.

Some time passed, and it became unbearable for the boy's parents to live without their son.

The father went once again to the spring, took a drink of water, and sighed, this time sadly, "Oh!"

Okhik immediately popped out of the water and said, "Why have you called me?"

"It's hard for us to live without our son. I have come to take him home so that he can help us with the chores," the father said.

"He still hasn't learned a trade," Okhik said.

"If that is the case, help us so that somehow we can make a living."

Okhik dove into the water and brought back a tablecloth. He gave the tablecloth to the boy's father and said, "Take this tablecloth. Whenever you want to eat, spread open the cloth and all sorts of food will appear."

The man took the tablecloth and returned to his village. At home he spread open the tablecloth, and all kinds of victuals actually did appear. From that day on the man and woman lived without want.

One day the woman said to her husband, "I want to invite the wife of the *melik** to our home."

"There's no need to invite the *melik*'s wife," said the man. "She'll see the tablecloth and take it away."

"All the same, I'm going to invite her to dinner."

"There's no need, I tell you. You'll be sorry."

The woman insisted on having her way and invited the *melik*'s wife and some neighbors to dinner.

When the guests arrived, they noticed that the hearth wasn't burning and that nothing had been prepared for dinner. "Why on earth did she invite us here?" they began whispering.

When the time came to have dinner, the woman got the tablecloth and spread it out on the table. All kinds of wonderful dishes appeared. The *melik*'s wife thought, "I'd like to steal the tablecloth." Turning around and seeing that the village elder was there, she whispered to him, "I have the exact same tablecloth at home. Run quickly and bring it here."

The village elder ran and got the tablecloth the woman had requested. When no one was looking, the *melik*'s wife exchanged her tablecloth for the magic tablecloth.

The guests departed. That evening when the peasant and his wife wanted to eat, they got the tablecloth and spread it out, but to their amazement nothing appeared. Then they understood that the *melik*'s wife had stolen their tablecloth.

The next day the man and his wife went to the spring. They took a drink and sighed, "Oh!"

Okhik popped up out of the water. "What do you want?" he asked.

"We are hungry," they replied.

"What did you do with the tablecloth I gave you?"

"The *melik*'s wife stole it."

Okhik dove into the water and brought them a gourd. "Take this gourd. If you shake it, a horse cavalry will jump out of the gourd, and they'll wage war against the *melik*."

The husband and wife took the gourd and returned to their village. Once they were at home, they shook the gourd. Armed horsemen began jumping out of the gourd. After getting into formation, they waged war on the *melik*. They began tearing down the walls, doors, and windows of the *melik*'s house.

The people who had gathered to see what was happening asked, "What is going on?"

"We came to take back the tablecloth that was stolen by the *melik*'s wife," the warriors answered.

The *melik* took fright and immediately gave the tablecloth to the horsemen, who in turn gave it to the rightful owner. The man hid the horse cavalry in the gourd and hung the gourd on the wall.

Several years passed. One day the peasant said, "Our son must have learned a trade by now. Let's go get him and bring him home."

They went to the spring, drank of its waters, and sighed, "Oh!"

Okhik appeared and asked why they had called on him.

"Give us our son," the parents begged. "Whether he knows a trade or not, enough is enough."

"I'll go have a look," said Okhik. "If I see that he knows a trade, I'll give him to you." And Okhik dove into the water.

Okhik had a daughter. She had become friends with the young man. "Do you see how many chopped-off heads there are here?" she asked. "These are the heads of my father's pupils. If Father asks you whether or not you have learned a trade, answer 'no.' Then he won't be able to chop off your head, too."

Okhik came to the boy and asked, "Well, lad, tell me, have you learned a trade yet? Your parents have come for you."

"No, master, I haven't learned anything yet."

Okhik began hitting the boy. He thrashed him and kept demanding that the boy say that he had learned something. The boy kept repeating "no." Understanding that his efforts were in vain, Okhik took the boy to his parents, who were very glad indeed to see their son.

"You go on ahead, and I'll catch up," said the lad.

The young man turned into a raven black horse. He caught up to his parents and galloped past them, grazing his father's shoulder. Then he turned back into a young man and went up to his father.

"Son, it's a shame that you lagged behind. While you were gone, a fiery horse galloped by. If you had been with us, we could have caught it."

While they were walking home, their son turned into ten different animals and ran past his parents.

After they had reached home, the young man said, "Father, the animals that ran past you—the horse, the doe, the reindeer, and all the other animals—were me. My trade is shape-shifting.

"If you like, I'll turn into a stallion. Take me to market and sell me. Just be sure that you sell me without selling the bridle, too. I will be the bridle, and if you sell it with the horse, I'll never return."

The boy turned into a raven black horse several times, and each time his father sold him without the bridle. Every evening the young man returned home, as if nothing had happened.

One day when the father sold his son in the guise of a horse, Okhik was at the market. He recognized his pupil as the horse. Recognizing the boy's father, too, Okhik approached him. The father didn't remember Okhik right away.

"How much do you want for the horse?" Okhik asked the father.

"A hundred and fifty," the father answered.

"But you must sell me the horse and the bridle."

"No, I'm selling the horse without the bridle."

"I'll give you two hundred, but you must give me the bridle with the horse," said Okhik.

The peasant was tempted, so he gave in. Okhik took the horse to the spring. He tied it to a post and said to his daughter, "Look after him. I'm going to get my bow and arrow so that I can kill him."

As soon as Okhik left, the girl freed the horse, which turned into a bird and flew away. When he saw what had happened, Okhik turned into a hawk and chased the bird.

Noticing a wedding taking place on earth below, the bird turned into a rose and fell among the wedding party. The hawk changed into an *ashug*, or folksinger. With his *saz*, a stringed instrument, in hand he approached the people attending the wedding feast. One by one, the guests began smelling the rose. When the *ashug*'s turn came to smell the rose, he took it and crushed it.

Just as he was going to stamp on the rose, the flower turned into a fistful of millet and sprinkled over the earth. A single grain fell into a guest's slipper. The *ashug* turned into a hen and chickens, and the hen and her chicks began pecking the grain.

But the grain that had gotten stuck in the guest's slipper turned into a fox. The fox killed the hen and chickens and turned back into a young man.

Three apples fell from heaven—one apple for the storyteller, the second for the person listening to the story, and the third apple for the whole, wide world.

---

*There were five hereditary *melik*s, or rulers, one for each of Armenia's five principalities in Karabakh.

FORTY THIEVES

*L*ong, long ago in ancient times there lived a man and wife who were so poor that it was impossible to be poorer. They had an only son. Wherever they apprenticed their son, whatever work he undertook, it was all in vain. He would stay with the master craftsman for a while and work a day or two, and then he would run home.

One day the lad said to his parents, "Let me apprentice with the tailor. Maybe I'll like tailoring. I'll learn the trade and go out into the world."

"Very well," said the boy's parents. "Let's give it a try and see what comes of it."

They took the boy to the tailor. But the tailor was no ordinary one, for this tailor sewed clothing for the king.

A day passed, a second day passed, and a third day passed. Then the king summoned the tailor and gave him a length of silk. "Sew me a robe," the king said, "but be careful not to spoil the silk, or it's off with your head!"

The tailor made a low bow, took the length of silk, and left. He went back to his shop. After placing the material on the table, he went home to have dinner.

The master craftsman had no sooner left his shop than his apprentice took a pair of scissors and cut the silk into little pieces. He cut up the cloth the way he saw fit.

The tailor returned in an hour. When he saw what his apprentice had done, his hair stood on end. "What have you done?" asked the tailor.

After uttering these words, he grabbed a stick with the intent of giving his pupil a good beating. But the pupil turned around, scampered out of the shop, and ran home.

At home his parents scolded him. "What can we do with you? What will happen to us now? You run away from everyone. You should have pity on us. Instead, you've exhausted us completely."

"Well, then, Father," said the son, "tomorrow buy some raisins. Fill the pockets of my robe, and you and I will set out on a trip. You'll apprentice me wherever we are when we run out of raisins to eat."

"All right," said the father. "We'll give it a try."

The next day the father took some bread for the trip and went with his son to the marketplace. There he bought several pounds of raisins. He filled his son's pockets, and father and son set out.

They walked for one, two, three hours. In short, they walked all day long. Toward evening they reached a wasteland. There they discovered that the son's raisins were all gone.

"Father, enroll me into an apprenticeship here," said the boy.

"To whom shall I give you? There is no one to be seen here," said the father.

No sooner had the boy's father spoken than someone appeared.

"Someone's coming!" the son said happily. "Let me be his apprentice."

"Hello," said the man who was approaching.

"Hello, may God help you," answered the father.

"Who are you? What are you doing here?" asked the man. "Neither a snake crawling on its belly nor a bird on the wing has come here in the past. What made you decide to come?"

"I want to apprentice my son. What is your trade, my friend?"

"We are forty thieves," the stranger answered. "At night we rob villages. In a word, we steal anything that isn't buttoned down. Now you know what our trade is. If you are agreed, give us your son, and we'll teach him our trade. Or don't give him to us. Do as you please."

"You know, Father, this is just what I need. Nothing could be better," said the useless son. "By robbing, I'll amass money and various treasures. I'll grow wealthy."

"As you wish, Son," said the father, "but watch out. If anything happens, you'll have only yourself to blame."

The father kissed his son on both cheeks. Then he took him by the hand and gave him to the thief. He bade his son farewell and went home.

The thief set out with the lad. Whether they traveled a long or short time is unknown, but eventually they came to a large stone.

"Do you see that stone?" asked the thief. "We live beneath it. Now we'll climb down under it, and you'll meet our ringleader. He sits at the most honored place. Approach and bow down to him. Then go sit by the door in the lowliest place."

"All right," said the lad, who was shaking with fear. "I'll do just that."

The thief lifted the stone, beneath which was a deep hole. They climbed down beneath the earth and went to the thief's palace. There the boy saw thieves who were armed from head to toe. He approached the ringleader, bowed low, and sat down near the door.

An hour passed. Then a second and a third hour passed. Suddenly, the ringleader shouted loudly, "Hey, I'd like a brave man to go to the bathhouse, prepare some *halvah** there, and bring it to me."

The boy was surprised that not one of the thieves moved from his place. So the boy stood up and said, "I'll go prepare *halvah* for you."

"Silence!" said the ringleader, becoming angry. "The boy is brave, but everyone else is silent. The boy alone has courage."

The boy sat down again. Another hour passed, and once again the ringleader shouted, "Hey, I'd like a brave man to go to the bathhouse, prepare some *halvah* for me, and bring it to me."

The thieves were as silent as they had been before.

The boy couldn't restrain himself. Once again he rose and shouted, "I'll go prepare *halvah* and bring it to you."

"Silence!" said the angry ringleader. "Why are you pestering me?"

Once again the poor lad sat down.

More time passed, and once again the ringleader cried, "I'd like a brave man to go to the bathhouse, prepare some *halvah*, and bring it to me."

Once again the thieves were silent.

Then, the boy couldn't bear it any longer. "What is difficult about it?" he asked. "Let me go prepare *halvah* for you."

"Well, all right," said the ringleader. "Show him where the bathhouse is, and let him prepare the *halvah* and bring it to me."

The thieves took some butter, sugar, and flour. They led the boy to a spot where the bathhouse could be seen in the distance. They pointed to it and returned to their den.

The boy went into the bathhouse and looked around. There wasn't a soul. He made a fire and put a frying pan on the fire.

After preparing the *halvah*, he grabbed the frying pan handle and started to leave. But he heard a voice calling him. The voice was emanating from the hole in the roof, through which the smoke escapes. It was a woman holding a wooden spoon. "Lad, oh lad, treat me to your *halvah*!"

"Give me your spoon," said the boy. He grabbed the spoon and scooped up some *halvah* and gave it to the woman. She ate it and asked for more. This happened three times. No matter how many times she asked, the lad didn't refuse.

Finally, the boy got tired of complying. He grabbed the frying pan and headed toward the door.

The woman called him again. "Lad, oh lad, come here. Let me place my foot on your back so that I can get down from the roof to wash."

The boy put down the frying pan and leaned over so that the woman could jump down onto his back. She used his back as a support and jumped down.

As soon as she was on firm ground, she attacked the boy in an attempt to topple him. The lad grappled with her. They fought until the boy threw her onto the ground. Shamed in battle, the woman jumped up and ran away. However, she left her small slipper behind on the floor.

The boy picked up the small slipper and looked at it. Pearls were sewn onto it, and it was so beautiful, so elegant, that he could do nothing but gaze at it.

The boy took the small slipper and the *halvah* and placed them before the ringleader.

"Brave lad!" the amazed ringleader cried. Getting up from his seat, the ringleader kissed the boy on the forehead. "For many years I have wanted *halvah*, but none of my band would go to the bathhouse to prepare it."

The ringleader placed the lad beside him in the place of honor.

One day, two days, three days—in short, a week passed. One day the ringleader said, "I want one of you to take this slipper to the marketplace and sell it. With the money you receive, buy everything that we need."

None of the thieves would undertake the task. Instead, they began trying to persuade the boy. "Only you know how to sell the slipper," they said.

"All right," the boy said. "If I have to, I'll go."

He took the slipper and set out for town. But no one at the marketplace wanted to buy the slipper. After all, who has need for a single slipper?

The boy walked around the marketplace. Finally, he saw the king's nazir, or official, coming toward him.

"Listen, lad, where did you get that slipper?" the nazir asked.

"What business is it of yours?" asked the boy. "If you want it, buy it. If you don't want it, go on your way."

"That is the queen's slipper," said the nazir. "Let's go to the king." He dragged the boy to the palace straight to the king.

"That is my wife's slipper," said the king, after looking it over. "How did you happen to come by it? Tell the truth, or I'll have your head chopped off."

"May God grant you a long life, oh king," answered the lad. "I found the slipper one day in a bathhouse." And he told the king what had happened.

"If that is so," the king said, "I won't release you until you bring me the other slipper."

"May God grant you a long life, oh king," said the boy. "How can I bring the other slipper to you if you won't release me? I have forty comrades. Give me some people of my own, and I'll bring my comrades here to be held hostage until I return. I'll go after the slipper, but give me forty days to complete the task. If I don't bring the slipper back in that amount of time, do whatever you want with me."

"Very well," said the king, "let it be as you wish."

He gave the lad his own guards, and they went to fetch the robbers. They brought all of the thieves to the king, who ordered that they be locked up in a room until the boy returned.

The lad got ready for his journey and left the palace quickly. He walked on for one, two, three days until he came to a village.

On the outskirts of the village, he met an old woman. She was standing at a grave with a stick in her hand. Suddenly, she struck the earth and commanded, "Open, earth!"

The earth opened, and there lay a corpse. The old woman struck the dead man and said, "Come to life!" The dead man revived.

The boy was amazed. He decided to take the magic wand away from the old woman. He crept up and grabbed the stick. The old woman wouldn't let go. She held on. A battle broke out. The boy defeated the old woman and took away her magic wand.

He traveled on. Only God knows how far he went. Finally, he came to a town, gleaming white. The town seemed deserted. No one was on the streets. There was no noise, no sound of a human voice. Finally, the boy noticed a man approaching him from the other end of the street.

The man drew nearer and said, "Brother traveler, neither a snake crawling on its belly nor a bird on the wing dares show itself in our town. How is it that you decided to come here? If the king finds out about it, he won't take it kindly."

"Why? What has happened here?" the boy asked.

"Nothing worse can happen to us now," answered the townsman. "It has been a year since our king's only son died. When his son got ill, the king summoned every doctor in the country. No matter what the doctors did, the king's son couldn't be cured. Finally, the king's son died. Our town has been in mourning for a year now. No one has the right to take a step in this town. If anyone does, the angry king will have his head chopped off."

"Where is the grave of the king's son?" asked the boy. "I'll revive him."

"Don't undertake that task, lad. Your life is still ahead of you. Leave and live a long, healthy life. Don't expose yourself to danger."

"No," said the boy, "it's none of your business. Take me to the king."

"As you like," the man said. He took the boy by the arm and led him to the king's palace. He left him at the gate while he went into the palace. The man bowed low and stood by the door to the king's chambers.

"What do you want?" the king asked angrily.

"May you live a long life, oh king," the man said. "A stranger, a young man, has come to town. He says that he can bring your son back to life."

"Where is the lad?" asked the king.

"He is waiting at the gate. If you give the order, I'll call him."

"Let him come in. Let's have a look and see who he is," answered the king.

The man went after the lad and led him to the king. The boy bowed low and stood by the door.

"Who are you?" the king asked. "Where are you going?"

"May your life be long, oh king! I came to bring your son back to life."

"You don't have a mouth, but rather a temple from which you utter holy words," said the king. "If you bring my son back to life, I'll give you much gold. But if you fail to bring him back to life, it's off with your head! Do you agree?"

"Agreed! If your son doesn't revive, you can kill me."

"Take him to my son's grave," commanded the king.

The nazirs, or officials, and viziers, or ministers of state, led him to the grave of the king's son. It was beside the palace. Meanwhile, the king went to the window. "I'll just see how he brings my son to life," he thought.

From beneath the folds of his robe, the boy took the old woman's wand. He struck the gravestone and said, "Move aside, stone!" The stone immediately moved aside.

Then the boy struck the earth and said, "Open wide, earth!"

The earth opened up, and the corpse of the king's son was visible.

Then the lad struck the corpse with the magic wand. "Arise, dead man!" he commanded.

Suddenly, before everyone's eyes, the king's son gave a sneeze. He sat up and stood at full height.

Overjoyed, the king jumped from the window and ran to his son, whom he embraced.

"Lad," cried the king, "ask for whatever you wish. I wouldn't begrudge you half my kingdom."

"May you live long, oh king," said the boy. "I don't need anything. Just order the captain of your ship to take me to the other side of the sea."

"Is that all you want?" asked the amazed king. "Ask me for gold or valuable wares. Ask for wealth. I won't begrudge you anything."

"No, king. You keep your wealth and use it to your heart's content. Just command that I be set down on the other shore. That's all I want."

For a long time, the king tried to persuade the boy to ask for something else, but he wouldn't. Then he commanded his ship's captain to appear before him. "Take this lad to the other shore in total safety," said the king.

"May you live long, oh king," said the captain. "It has been a month since our ship has been able to travel to the other shore. As soon as we get to the middle of the sea, such a storm arises that it sinks the ship. I don't understand what is going on."

"No matter what happens, I have to travel to the other side of the sea, even if it means that I become food for the fish," said the boy.

"As you wish," said the captain. "You'll have only yourself to blame."

The captain got ready for the journey. He readied the ship and set out for sea with the boy. They sailed on. Whether they sailed for a long or short time, only God knows. Eventually, they reached the middle of the sea. There a terrible storm arose, which began hurling the vessel about on the waves so that it almost overturned.

It was then that our brave young man took off his clothing and jumped into the sea. He dove to the bottom of the sea. There he found an old woman with a ring on her finger. When she turned the stone of the ring in one direction, the sea became agitated and raged. When she turned the stone in the opposite direction, the sea became calm.

The lad immediately attacked the old woman and grabbed her by the throat. He took the ring from her finger and swam to the surface.

There was no longer a storm. The captain didn't know what to think. They sailed on. They sailed for one, two, three days—in short, they sailed on for a week. Finally, they moored the ship to shore. The boy bid farewell to the captain and set out for the interior of the country.

He traveled on until he reached a large magic garden. He went into the garden. A palace stood in the heart of the garden. It was so beautiful that one could neither eat, nor drink, but had to stare only at it. The lad walked straight to the palace.

He opened the palace door and entered the first chamber. There he found a table covered with delicious dishes of the sort that only God could have created. The young man was hungry and immediately attacked the food. But no sooner had he taken a piece of bread than the bread turned back to grain and scattered on the floor. He picked up a roasted chicken, and the chicken came alive. He touched a boiled fish, and suddenly it began wriggling and slipped from his hands. In short, whatever he touched came alive and scattered or slipped from his hands.

"Well," said the lad, "something's not right here. It's the work of evil spirits."

He glanced around and noticed a large stove with a drawn curtain. "I'll hide there. I'll sit and watch how this turns out," he thought, and he hid behind the curtain near the stove.

The boy had been sitting for one, two, three hours when suddenly three white doves flew into the room. They cast off their feathers and turned into maidens as beautiful as the *peri*.**

The maidens went up to the table to dine. The plates were on the floor, and the food was scattered here and there. Everything in the chamber was topsy-turvy.

"Someone was here," the maidens said. "Someone touched everything and turned over everything that was on the table. Who could it be? Who decided to enter our palace?"

They gave the question a great deal of thought and searched everywhere. Finally, they got tired and sat down.

"Oh, I know," said the eldest sister to the middle sister. "Perhaps it's the lad who prepared *halvah* in the bathhouse and fought with me. He took my slipper and left. If he were here, I would kiss him to my heart's content. And you and our youngest sister would treat him with affection. And then once again I would. . . ."

"Oh, I know," said the middle sister to the eldest. "Perhaps it's the lad who attacked me when I was bringing a dead man back to life. He hit me on the head, tore the magic wand from my hands, and went away. If he were here, I would kiss him to my heart's content. And you and our youngest sister would treat him with affection. And once again I . . . ."

"Oh, I know," said the youngest sister to the eldest. "Perhaps he is the lad who dove to the bottom of the sea. He took my ring and hid. If he were here, I would kiss him to my heart's content. And you and our middle sister would treat him with affection. And once again I . . . ."

The young man sitting behind the curtain heard the conversation. "Aren't these the maidens I have been seeking while wandering over hill and dale?" he thought, and he came out from behind the curtain.

When the sisters saw him, they were happy. They rushed to kiss him all at the same time. They kissed and kissed and couldn't get their fill. Finally, they sat down and ate and drank. They conversed sweetly and couldn't talk enough.

"To this day neither a snake crawling on its belly nor a bird on the wing has decided to set foot here. Tell us, how did you come to visit us?" asked the sisters.

"Love led me to you," the lad answered.

"May you always have love," said the maidens. "But now tell us the whole truth."

"If I hide something from you, I can't hide it from God." And the lad told the sisters what had happened to him.

"Tomorrow the time limit is up," he said. "If I don't get the other slipper to the king, he'll order his men to chop off my comrades' heads."

"Don't worry," said the sisters. "You have a great deal of time. You'll no sooner glance around than you'll be there."

"Thank you," said the young man. "I'll never forget your kindness."

"Rest assured," said the maidens, "that tonight we'll sew a slipper that will please your soul, and you'll take it to the king. Only, tell us when you will return, for now we are yours and you are ours."

"Give me three days," said the lad. "If I don't return in three days, you'll know that I'm in trouble."

"Fine," said the sisters. "We'll give you three days."

In one night the sisters sewed 300 slippers. They rose early in the morning and prepared supplies for the trip. They filled a leather sack with the slippers and turned into doves. After seating the lad on their wings, they flew off.

They flew an entire day, and only toward evening did they descend in the vicinity of the king's palace. The lad took the leather sack and hurried to the palace in the nick of time. The executioners had already gathered to chop off his comrades' heads.

The lad entered the palace and placed the leather sack before the king. "May you have a long life, king," said the young man. "Have a look. Instead of one slipper, I've brought you a sack full of them."

Slippers were scattered before the king, whose mouth hung open in amazement. The king commanded that the forty thieves be released. After giving them gifts, the king set them free to go wherever they pleased.

The forty thieves didn't know how to thank the lad. After explaining that he had to leave because pressing matters awaited him, the young man parted from them.

The lad went into a field and tracked down the doves.

"Where do you want to fly now?" asked the sisters.

"To my parents'," answered the young man. "We'll get them and then fly to your country."

"All right," said the maidens. "Let's go."

They seated the lad on their wings and shot into the air. They flew on until they finally reached the lad's home, where they alighted at the door of the house.

When the lad's parents saw him, their joy knew no bounds. "Where were you for so long, Son?" they asked.

The young man sat down and told his parents everything that had happened. He told them that he wanted them to go with him to the land of the doves. The parents gave everything they owned to neighbors and relatives. The next morning they left the house. Each person sat on a dove's back and flew to the doves' palace.

Only God knows whether they flew for a long or short time, but finally they reached the magic garden. The doves lowered their precious cargo onto the earth, and the palace gates opened before them. Then the doves cast off their feathers and once again turned into three beautiful maidens.

They prepared for a wedding, and the young man married the sister of his choice. The wedding feast lasted seven days and seven nights. The celebrants danced to the music of the *zurna*.*** They ate and drank and enjoyed themselves so much that there was no end to their merriment.

They attained their happiness. May you attain your happiness, too.

Halvah is an Eastern candy made of caramel, nuts, and honey.

**In ancient Persian mythology the *peri* was a spirit descended from fallen angels and not permitted into paradise. More recently, the *peri* was thought to be a beautiful, benevolent fairy. In Greek mythology the *peri* is an oread, or nymph of mountains and caves.

***The *zurna* is a wooden wind musical instrument that sounds similar to the clarinet or bugle. It is traditionally played at weddings and festivals.

GAMBAR

*T*here once lived a woman who had only one son. His name was Gambar. The mother and son lived in dire poverty. Every day Gambar took a rope and went to the field to gather thorns and couch grass, which he took to market and sold for almost nothing. He bought bread with the money he made.

One day Gambar carried his couch grass to the square in front of the king's palace. The king's daughter glanced out the window at Gambar, who was dressed in rags. "The poor lad. If he had a wife, do you think he would go about looking so ragged?" the princess asked her father.

The king got angry at his daughter's comment, but he uttered not a word. He summoned his nazirs, or officials, and his viziers, or ministers of state. "Go call the peddler of couch grass to me," he ordered.

The nazirs and viziers went to fetch Gambar. Gambar was frightened. He couldn't understand what the king wanted of him. He entered the palace, bowed to the king, and stood to the side.

"Hey, there, lad," the king said. "I called you here to give you my daughter in marriage. Will you marry her?"

Gambar was dumbfounded. Had he heard right?

Then the king's daughter spoke. "Listen, lad, why are you so perplexed? If my parents have given their daughter to you, what are you afraid of? Marry me."

The wedding was celebrated for seven days and seven nights. Afterward, Gambar took the king's daughter and brought her to his home.

When they entered Gambar's humble home, Gambar said to his mother, "Mom, the king gave me his daughter in marriage. Here is your daughter-in-law. Set up a comfortable place for her, and let her sit down."

The house reeked of poverty. The walls were blackened from the dung they burned for heat. There was dirt everywhere. There wasn't even a small, cheap rug. There were only two goatskins, and they were in tatters. But Gambar's mother had patched them, just as she had patched all of their clothing. Gambar's mother took one of the tattered goatskins and set it out for the king's daughter to sit upon.

The king's daughter sat down and looked around. She gave thanks to God. "Evidently, this is my fate," she thought.

The king's daughter tore off a piece of her own dress to patch Gambar's clothing. Then she washed his clothing and tidied up.

The next day Gambar went to the field again to collect thorns and couch grass, and once again he took his wares to the square in front of the king's palace to sell them. The king looked out the window and saw that Gambar's clothing wasn't as shabby as it had been before.

When Gambar returned home that evening and his wife saw that his hands were pricked and bleeding because of the thorns he sold, her heart ached with pity. "Listen, she said to him, "this is no way to live. All day long you toil among rough rocks and quicksand. You crawl like a snake and drink water from the frog swamp, and all in vain. Your only profit is a few coins. Wouldn't it be better to seek another trade? Go to work for someone else as a servant. Work as a hired hand. Maybe something will come along."

"Very well, wife. I'll do as you wish," Gambar said.

At dawn Gambar arose and went to the marketplace. "I'll hire myself out as a laborer, or I'll work for someone for a month or two," he thought.

He walked around the marketplace asking first one, then another, person for work.

Suddenly, a merchant approached Gambar and asked, "Hey, lad, will you work for me?"

"Why not," replied Gambar. "That's why I came here. And how much will you pay me for working for you for a year?"

"If you make a profit honestly, I'll give you one measure of gold. If you make a profit dishonestly, I'll give you two measures of gold."

"Very well. I'll discuss this with my wife," said Gambar.

The young man returned home and told his wife, "A merchant wants to hire me and promised to pay me one measure of gold for making a profit honestly and two measures of gold for making a profit dishonestly. I don't know what to do."

"Don't agree to make a profit dishonestly, even if he promises you ten measures of gold. Take the one measure he promised for honest work."

"All right then, I'll go to work for the merchant. He is getting ready to journey to far-away lands to purchase goods."

After saying good-bye to his wife, Gambar went to the merchant. "Hello there, merchant. Pay me the one measure of gold for making a profit honestly, and I'll work for you."

"Very well," said the merchant, "let it be your way."

Gambar prepared for the journey. He bound the bales of supplies, loaded the bales onto mules, and set out with the merchant.

They traveled on for a long time and finally came to a wasteland. "Let's stop beside this well," said the merchant. "The mules will eat and drink. We'll have something to eat, too, and we'll rest for a while ourselves."

They unloaded the mules and started eating. After they were done, the merchant asked, "Can you descend into the well to fetch water for the mules?"

"I can," answered Gambar.

The merchant tied a rope around Gambar's waist and lowered him into the well. Gambar scooped up water and passed it up until all of the mules had been given a drink.

"Now let down the rope and pull me up," Gambar shouted from the well.

The rope was lowered into the well. When Gambar went to tie the rope around his waist, someone grabbed him by his robe and wouldn't let go. Gambar was amazed. He turned and saw two open doors at the bottom of the well. He looked through one door and saw a heap of headless corpses lying there. He looked through the other door and saw a heap of chopped-off heads. Three maidens of unearthly beauty were sitting there, sewing on lace frames. A frog was seated beside them on a silver tray. Beside the frog a handsome young man was seated. The young man couldn't take his eyes off the frog.

"Lad, tell us the truth. Which one of us is more beautiful—we three maidens or the speckled frog? Why is that young man staring at the frog? Why can't he take his eyes off her?" asked the maidens.

"What can I say?" replied Gambar. "One who is beloved always seems to be more beautiful."

No sooner had he uttered these words than the frog split apart and threw off her skin. The frog turned into a maiden of such beauty that she eclipsed the other three young women.

"What is the meaning of this? And what are these corpses and heads?" Gambar asked the handsome young man.

"Brother, I have been sitting in this well for forty years," said the young man. "Many people have been here, but not one was able to answer as you did, 'One who is beloved always seems to be more beautiful.' We chopped off their heads because they gave silly answers."

The handsome young man turned to the maidens and said, "Now give this lad a reward for answering so wisely."

Each of the three maidens brought a ripe pomegranate to Gambar. They just managed to pass the pomegranates to Gambar when the door slammed so that Gambar was left standing in the well again.

Gambar put the pomegranates in his pocket and shouted, "Pull me up now."

The merchant was glad when he heard Gambar's voice. He began thanking the Lord God that his servant had managed to get out of the well safe and sound. You see, the merchant had hired forty servants, and one after another they had disappeared in the well.

Part 3: Fairy Tales

Gambar was raised on the rope. He told the merchant nothing about what he had seen and heard in the well. He loaded the mules again and set out.

The hired man and his master rode on until they met up with another caravan. The caravan was headed to Gambar's native land. Gambar recognized a fellow villager among the muleteers. "Where are you headed?" asked Gambar.

"To our village," the muleteer answered.

"Then do me the kindness of taking these three pomegranates. Give them to my wife," said Gambar.

"That is no trouble at all. Give them to me, and I'll take them to her," said the lad. He took the pomegranates and put them in his bosom. Bidding farewell, the muleteer went on his way. The caravan set out in one direction, and Gambar set out in the opposite direction.

While they are on their journey, let's return to Gambar's wife. She was pregnant and yearned for a taste of pomegranate, but she had no means of obtaining one.

Suddenly, there was a knock at the gate. Gambar's wife went out and saw the neighbor's son standing there.

"Hello, little sister," the boy said. "Take these pomegranates. I met Gambar while I was on my journey, and he told me to give these pomegranates to you. He is alive and well and sends you his love."

Gambar's wife took the pomegranates and went into the house.

"I'll cut a pomegranate open and see how it tastes," she thought.

She cut into the pomegranate, and what did she see? The pomegranate was full of diamonds and pearls. In short, there was every conceivable precious stone in the pomegranate.

Gambar's wife was so happy that she didn't know where to begin using the fortune she found inside the pomegranate. After all, the house was such a poor one.

Immediately, she took a precious stone to the marketplace to the moneychanger. She sold it, and with the money she got for it, she bought something for the house. Little by little she took the rest of the stones to the marketplace and sold them. She bought a new house and decorated it. She bought cows and sheep. She prepared everything for Gambar's return. Soon she gave birth to a son, who was admired by everyone.

Now let's leave her and return to Gambar. The caravan of Gambar's merchant traveled on and finally reached the country in which the merchant's home was located. Ultimately, Gambar served the merchant for seventeen long years.

One day the merchant said to Gambar, "Get ready for a journey, Gambar. I have to go after some wares again."

When Gambar heard these words, he was glad. He could scarcely feel the feet beneath him. "We'll have to travel through my village. I'll probably be able to drop in at home and see my wife."

Gambar got ready for the journey. After he tied the bales and loaded the mules, they set out. Whether they traveled for a long or short time, only God knows. They traveled day and night until they reached the well into which they had lowered Gambar to fetch water. Again Gambar descended into the well and got water for the mules, but no beautiful maidens were there, no open doors. There was no one and nothing in the well. The caravan rested beside the well.

After eating, they set out. They traveled one, two, three days. In short, they traveled a week until they finally reached the border of Gambar's country.

There they took the bales off the mules in order to rest a while and have a bite to eat. Then they set out again. They came upon a great flock of sheep that were grazing.

Gambar approached the flock. "Hello, my friend," he said to the shepherd.

"May God protect you, traveler," the shepherd answered.

"What village are you from?" asked Gambar. "Are you from the village of Berd?"*

"I am."

"Have you heard of Gambar, the wanderer? Perhaps you know something about his family."

"Why wouldn't I know? This is his flock, and I am his shepherd."

"Whose shepherd are you?" the amazed Gambar asked.

"I am the shepherd of the seller of couch grass, to whom the king gave his daughter in marriage in a moment of anger."

Gambar was lost in thought. "What was the meaning of this? Who is this wealthy Gambar? About whom was the shepherd speaking?"

Gambar walked away from the shepherd and returned to the caravan. After eating, they loaded the mules and set out for Gambar's village.

On the way, they came upon a flock of sheep and a herd of cows. Gambar asked one person after another, "Whose flock is this? Whose herd is this?"

Everyone answered, "It's Gambar's."

Gambar marveled. "What is the meaning of this?" he wondered. "Could my wife have grown so wealthy that she has acquired a farm this big?" He pondered these events as he walked down the road.

Finally the caravan came to Gambar's village. Gambar asked his master's permission to visit home.

"Go ahead," the merchant said.

Gambar was happy. He hurried to his street and walked up and down it, but he couldn't find his house. He passed up and down the street ten times, but still he couldn't find his house. On the place where his old home had stood, there was a house of unprecedented beauty.

"I'll ask at this house," he thought. "Perhaps I'll find out about my wife."

Part 3: Fairy Tales

He entered the yard and saw his wife sitting at the window. A nice-looking boy was beside her. They were conversing peacefully. Gambar approached the window to overhear their conversation.

"Oh, my child, light of my eyes, if only your father would return and see how big you have grown, he would be so happy," his wife said to the boy.

"Mother, from childhood on you've spoken only of Father, but he's never here. I've worn my eyes out watching for him."

"God is merciful, my son. If your father is in good health, he will return someday."

Gambar could stand it no longer. He went into the house. Mother and son froze to the spot. They looked at one another.

"Don't you recognize me? I am Gambar."

As soon as he uttered these words, mother and son rushed to embrace him. Gambar's wife wept from happiness. It took her a long time to compose herself. They sat down and conversed affectionately. Gambar's wife set the table, and they ate and drank and thanked God.

"Listen, wife, where did this wealth come from?" asked Gambar. "How did you build a house like this? And how did you acquire herds of cows and flocks of sheep?"

"I cut open one of the three pomegranates that you sent me, and it was full of pearls and diamonds and other precious stones. I took the stones to the moneychanger in the marketplace, where I sold them. I built this house and stocked the farm with the money that I received."

Gambar's wife brought the second pomegranate to him. Gambar cut it open, and what did he see? It, too, was full of precious stones, pearls, and diamonds. He was so overjoyed that he couldn't feel his legs beneath him. Then he sat down and told his wife everything that had happened to him.

"If this is the situation, wife, why should I continue to serve the merchant? I'll go to him and ask him to find another worker."

"Of course," said his wife. "We have endured enough. How many days and nights have I spent yearning for you? How many black days have I seen? Let's live for ourselves now, comfortably and peacefully."

Gambar went to the merchant. "Master, give me my pay. I want to work for myself now."

"Do as you wish," said the merchant. "You have served me honestly for many years. I can't complain. If you no longer wish to stay with me, it is your business. May God be with you."

The merchant paid Gambar everything that he was supposed to and released him.

Gambar bid the merchant farewell and went home joyfully.

After arriving at home, he asked his wife, "Tell me, wife, after I left, did your father, the king, inquire about you? Did he take an interest in how you were living?"

"No, he didn't," replied Gambar's wife. "He's obstinate. He didn't ask about me even once. But I thought that as soon as you returned we would invite Father and his nazirs and viziers to our home. Who knows, maybe he thinks that we have died of hunger."

"That is a good idea, wife. Make the preparations. Tomorrow we'll invite the king to dinner."

"Call on him to invite him," said Gambar's wife. "Perhaps he won't recognize us."

Gambar's wife was delighted. She set about preparing for the king's visit in a lively manner. Thank goodness she had everything in the house. It took her no time at all to prepare a splendid feast.

The next day Gambar went to the king to invite him to dine with him. The king and his nazirs and viziers arrived at Gambar's home and were regaled splendidly. They ate and drank and feasted.

At the height of the merriment, Gambar's wife asked the king, "My Lord, it is said that you had a daughter. What became of her?"

"Oh, yes," said the king. "There was a peddler of thorns and couch grass. My daughter took a fancy to him. I got angry and gave her to him in marriage. Now when I remember my daughter, I am seized with melancholy. I ruined her with my own hands. I mourn over her with tears. Now I repent. I beat my head on the wall, all in vain. I don't even know if she is still alive or if she has died of hunger. Oh, if only I could see her again, my grief would be less!"

Gambar's wife could bear it no longer. She rushed to her father and embraced him. "I am your daughter," she said. "Don't you recognize me? This is my son, and this is my husband, the couch grass peddler. I told you that he was an intelligent man, but you didn't believe me. Now do you see how much wealth he has amassed with honest labor?"

The king marveled. Unable to believe his eyes, he looked at them. And it seemed to him that it was all a dream.

They began feasting again. The merriment began with the music of the *dap* and the *zurna*.** They celebrated until morning.

They had to wait for their happiness, but their story ended joyfully, as will your story.

_____

*The name of the village was selected at random because in typical fairytale manner the text does not name a specific village.

**Musical instruments.

THE BEARDLESS SORCERER AND THE KING'S SON

*T*here once lived a king who had two sons. One day the king summoned his sons and his nazirs, or officials, and viziers, or ministers of state, and said, "My time is up. I am going to die. But while I am still alive, I want to write a testament with my own hand. I bequeath my kingdom to my older son and my cat and rooster to my younger son."

After speaking, the king gave up his soul to God. His sons buried him as he had desired and returned home. The older son sat upon the throne and began ruling the country.

One day the younger brother came to the older brother and said, "Brother, I've lived in your care long enough. Give me my inheritance, and I'll devote my attention to my own affairs."

"Brother, what does it matter what Father bequeathed us?" said the older brother. "Live with me, and we'll rule the country together. We'll live our time out in peace and prosperity."

The younger brother refused the offer. "No, I must fulfill our father's bidding."

The older brother saw that he couldn't persuade his younger brother, so he gave him his inheritance, the rooster and the cat, and accompanied him to the road.

The younger brother took the rooster and the cat and set out. Whether he traveled for a long or short time, only God knows. He traveled one day, two days, a week, two weeks—in short, he traveled an entire month. Finally, he came to a village. On the edge of the village, he met a beardless man.

"Hello, member of the king's family," said the beardless man. "Why are you visiting our part of the world?"

"Hello, Beardless, my friend. I'm just wandering around," answered the king's son.

"If that's the case, come visit me. You'll have a bite to eat and you'll rest for a while. Then you can be on your way again."

The king's son wanted to refuse the offer, but Beardless pestered him so that he finally agreed. They went to the home of Beardless. It so happened that Beardless was a sorcerer, and he knew that a talisman was hidden in the rooster that belonged to the king's son. "How can I slaughter that rooster and extract the talisman?" he wondered.

Beardless called his son aside and said, "Son, at dinner I'll give you a poke. When I do so, scream with all your might and demand that our guest's rooster be slaughtered. Do you understand?"

"Understood," replied the boy. "I'll do what you say."

Beardless called his wife and said, "Feed us. Our guest is on a long journey. He's probably hungry and tired. He'll have a bite to eat and a little rest after dinner."

Beardless's wife laid the table. She brought bread, a yogurt called *madzoon* in Armenian, everything that was in the house, and she placed it on the table. The family sat down and ate. Beardless's little son put his hand in the yogurt, smeared it all over himself, and then wiped his hand on his shirt. He did it once, twice, until Beardless could stand it no longer. The sorcerer swung his arm and slapped his son in the face.

The son raised such a howl that you'd think his legs had been chopped off. No matter how his mother and father tried to comfort him, no matter what they said, he wouldn't quiet down.

"Son, tell us what to give you to quiet you down. Your howling is making my head ache," said Beardless.

"I want chicken!" screamed the son.

His mother went to the yard and slaughtered a hen. She brought it to the boy. But her son didn't stop howling.

"Well, what else do you want?" his father asked. "You wanted chicken, and Mother slaughtered a hen. What else can we give you?"

"I want rooster meat. Slaughter our guest's rooster."

The king's son was tired of hearing the boy howl. He said, "What good is the rooster to me? Slaughter it, and perhaps the child will calm down."

That is just what Beardless wanted to hear. He slaughtered the rooster, and his son quieted down.

"Wife," said Beardless. "Make *arisa** for our dear guest. We'll entertain him till dawn, and then we'll send him on his way."

The woman plucked some hens as the king's son watched. She cleaned and washed them. Then she placed them in a pot. She heated the *tonir*, or oven, and cooked the *arisa*.

At dawn as soon as he heard the church bells ringing, Beardless set out for church. It was Beardless's custom to go to martins and vespers every day.

The king's son awoke and began preparing to continue his journey. He saw that Beardless wasn't at home. "Little sister, equip me for my journey. I don't have time to wait for Beardless to return," the king's son said to Beardless's wife.

For a long time, Beardless's wife prevailed upon the king's son to stay. She wanted to regale him with her *arisa*.

But the king's son wouldn't agree to stay. "No, I must leave," he insisted.

"If that's the case, I'll take some cooked chicken out of the pot and give it to you for your journey," said Beardless's wife.

Beardless's wife scooped into the pot and caught hold of the rooster. She pulled out the cooked rooster, rolled it up in a flat bread called lavash, and gave it to the king's son. The king's son bid Beardless's wife farewell and went on his way.

While the king's son goes his way, we'll turn our attention to Beardless. As soon as martins ended, Beardless returned home. "Where is our guest?" he asked his wife.

"He left. No matter how much I tried to persuade him, he wouldn't stay. He kept repeating, 'I don't have time.'"

"Did you give him something to take on his journey?"

"Certainly. I felt sorry for the poor man. We have so many hens, and we slaughtered his rooster."

Beardless rushed to the kettle of *arisa*. He dipped in a spoon and swished it around, but there was no rooster to be found.

He ran to his wife and shouted, "What have you done?"

Then he ran off in pursuit of his guest.

While Beardless pursues the king's son, we'll see what the king's son is doing. After traveling a distance, the king's son came to a cold, babbling spring. "I'll sit by this spring and have a bite to eat and a little rest. Then I'll be on my way," he thought.

He sat down by the spring, unfolded his tablecloth, and began eating. He ate the rooster and even gobbled up the rooster's bones. He noticed that a rusty ring was caught in the rooster's wishbone.

The king's son placed the ring on his finger. From nowhere two Arabs appeared before him.

"What is your command, King's Son?" they asked.

The young man was amazed. "Where could these Arabs have come from?" he wondered.

Then the king's son came to his senses and said, "Take me to such-and-such a kingdom."

The Arabs seated him on their shoulders and took him where he wanted. They set him down on the ground and disappeared.

The king's son traveled on. He saw a village in the distance, but dusk was already drawing near. "I'll just go have a look and see what's interesting there," he thought.

As he was walking down the village street, he came upon an old woman who was sitting by her gate spinning. "Hello, little mother," said the king's son.

"May God bless you, son. Where are you going so late this evening?"

"I don't know, little mother. I am a homeless wanderer. I'm alone. Won't you adopt me as your son?"

"Why not?" replied the old woman. "I don't have a son. Now that I am old, there is no one to look after me or give me a hand when I have bad luck. There's no one to pull splinters from my fingers."

"If that is the case, I will be your son, and you will be my mother."

"Very well, Son," said the old woman. She led the king's son into her home. Thereafter, mother and son lived in love and harmony.

One day the adopted son went to his mother and said, "Mother, I want to talk to you about something, but I don't know how you'll react."

"Speak, Son, speak."

"I want you to arrange a marriage between me and the daughter of the king of this country. What do you say to that?"

"Oh, woe is me! Have you lost your mind? How is that possible? We don't have enough bread to eat. How could you marry the king's daughter? Nothing good will come of this. The king will order our heads to be chopped off. What then?"

"If you won't arrange the marriage, I'll leave and go wherever my eyes gaze," the king's son said.

Mother and son quarreled for a long time. Finally the mother gave in and set out for the king's palace. She arrived and sat down on the matchmaker's stone beside the king's gate.

When the nazirs, or officials, and viziers, or ministers of state, saw the old woman, they went up to her and asked, "Would you please tell us why you have come?"

"I have come to the king with a request," said the old woman.

The nazirs and viziers went to inform the king. "My Lord, an old woman wants to see you. Shall we admit her?"

"Let her come in," said the king. "We'll see what the old woman wants."

The nazirs and viziers got the old woman and led her into the palace to the king. The old woman placed her hands on her chest and bowed low to the king.

"Well, what do you want, old woman?" asked the king.

"Hello, Your Majesty," said the old woman. "I have a request, but I dare not say what it is."

"Speak, speak. Let's hear what your request is."

"Your Majesty, I have a son. I've come to ask for your daughter's hand in marriage to him. It's up to you. If you want, give her to my son in marriage. If you don't want to, don't give her. You know best. We are ready to die for you, as you know."

"I'll give her to your son. Why not? But first you must fulfill my wish. If you fulfill my wish, everything will be fine. If you fail, it's off with both your heads. Agreed?"

"Agreed," sighed the old woman.

"In a single night you must build a palace for my daughter that is no worse than mine. It must be so beautiful that it takes one's breath away. If you build it, my daughter is yours. If you don't build it, neither you, nor your son, will have heads on your shoulders. Is that understood?"

"It's understood, Your Majesty," said the old woman, and she exited the king's palace.

Saddened, she arrived home.

"Well, how did it go?" asked her son. "Were you at the king's?"

"I was."

"What did the king say to you?"

"Oh, Son, the king wants what it is impossible to do."

"Never fear, Mother. Why are you so sad? Just tell me what the king wants."

"The king said, 'In a single night you must build a palace for my daughter that is no worse than mine.' How is that possible, Son?"

"Don't be sad, Mother. By tomorrow the palace will be ready."

After uttering these words, the young man put the rooster's ring on his finger. In the blink of an eye, the Arabs appeared.

"What do you command, King's Son?" they asked.

"Build a palace," said the lad, "that is so beautiful that it takes one's breath away. Build a palace that has no equal in the whole, wide world. It must be ready by dawn."

"Your wish will be fulfilled," said the Arabs, and they disappeared.

The old woman awoke at dawn. She opened her eyes, and what did she see? She was lying in stately chambers. She looked around and couldn't understand where she was. The poor woman had never seen anything like it, even in a dream. She guessed that her son had built the palace she found herself in, and she rejoiced.

"Well, Mother, do you like the palace?" her son asked. "Now go quickly and bring back the king's daughter."

"I'm going, Son. Now the king will have to give you his daughter's hand in marriage."

The old woman got dressed. She washed and combed her hair and tied a festive kerchief around her head. Then she set out for the king's palace. Once again she sat on the matchmaker's stone by the palace gate.

As he looked out the window, the king noticed the old woman. He guessed that she had come for his daughter. His servants announced that the palace was ready and that it was so splendid that whoever looked at it oohed and aahed.

The king sent for his nazirs and viziers and ordered them to bring the old woman to him. The nazirs and viziers did as he had commanded.

"I see that your son has built a splendid palace in a night," said the king. "But that isn't all that I want. I have another wish."

The Beardless Sorcerer and the King's Son

"Speak, Your Majesty. What is it that you desire?"

"Weave me a carpet that extends from my palace to the church, and from the church to your palace. Place green willows on either side of the carpet, and place singing birds in the willow branches to entertain my daughter. Do you understand my command?"

"I understand, Your Majesty," said the old woman. She bowed to the king and left the palace.

When she arrived home, she waited for her son to come home. When the king's son walked into the palace, he saw that once again his mother was sad.

"What happened, Mother?"

"Oh, Son, this time the king has thought up an impossible task."

"Tell me what the king wants."

"He wants a carpet that extends from his palace to the church, and from the church to our palace. He wants green willows growing on either side of the carpet, and he wants singing birds placed in the willow branches to entertain his daughter. Is this possible to do, Son?"

"Don't be sad, Mother. There will be such a carpet. Then we'll see what else the king wants."

Having uttered these words, the king's son put the rooster's ring on his finger. The Arabs appeared before him.

"What do you want, King's Son?" asked the Arabs.

"I want a carpet that extends from the king's palace to the church, and from the church to my palace. I want green willows growing on both sides of the carpet, and I want birds singing in the trees' branches. Do you understand?"

"We understand, King's Son," said the Arabs, and they disappeared.

After it got dark, the mother and son lay down to sleep. At dawn the sweet singing of birds reached the king's ears. The king was moved by their singing. "I'll get up and see if I can find out where the birds are singing so sweetly," thought the king.

The king walked out of the palace and saw a road extending from his palace to the church, and the road was covered with a carpet. Green willows were on either side of the road, and in the branches of the willows nightingales were singing so beautifully that the singing caused one's head to spin. The king didn't want to eat or drink or dress. He wanted only to stroll on the carpet and listen to the singing of the nightingales. That is how beautiful his surroundings had become.

"Yes, indeed," said the king. "The old woman certainly will take away my daughter. I must make a wish that is absolutely impossible to fulfill."

Meanwhile, the old woman and her son awoke to the sweet singing of the nightingales. "Well, Mother, the road and carpet are ready," said the young man. "Go bring me the king's daughter."

"I'm going," the old woman answered joyfully.

She dressed quickly, combed her hair, and tied a festive kerchief around her head. Off she went to the king's palace. After she arrived, she sat down on the matchmaker's stone. When the nazirs and viziers saw her, they led her straight to the king. The old woman bowed to the king and remained standing.

"What do you want, old woman?" asked the king. "Have you come for my daughter?"

"For your daughter, Your Majesty."

"You have fulfilled two of my wishes, but one still remains. If you fulfill that wish, you may take my daughter."

"Speak, Your Majesty. What is your third wish?"

"Make a wedding gown for my daughter that hasn't been sewn with needle and thread and that hasn't been cut with scissors. Do you understand?"

"I understand, Your Majesty," said the old woman. She made a low bow and left. She dragged herself home.

"Well, how did it go, Mother," asked her son. "What did the king say?"

"Oh, Son," said the old woman, "this time the king has thought up something so fantastic that I can't get it into my head."

"Tell me what he wants, Mother."

"He said, 'Bring a wedding dress for my daughter that hasn't been sewn with needle and thread and hasn't been cut with scissors.' How can we find such a wedding gown?"

"Don't grieve, Mother. There will be a wedding gown like that, and then we'll see what the king says."

After saying this, the king's son put the rooster's ring on his finger. The Arabs appeared again.

"What is your desire, King's Son?" asked the Arabs.

"Get me a maiden's wedding gown that hasn't been sewn with needle and thread and hasn't been cut with scissors. Do you understand?"

"Your wish will be fulfilled," said the Arabs, and they disappeared.

At dawn the son said, "Mother, go to the king's palace. The king's daughter must be already wearing the wedding gown."

"All right, I'll go."

The old woman got dressed. She combed her hair and put on her festive kerchief. Then she set out for the king's palace.

After arriving, she sat down on the matchmaker's stone. The nazirs and viziers saw her and summoned her to go to see the king. The old woman saw the king's daughter sitting beside him, dressed in a wedding gown so extraordinary that no pen could describe it. One wanted neither to eat, nor drink, but only to gaze at the king's daughter and her gown, so beautiful were they.

"Old woman, take my daughter," said the king. "Bring your son here, and we'll marry them."

The old woman hurried home. "Get up, Son! The king has summoned you. He said, 'Let him come, and I'll give him my daughter's hand in marriage.'"

"Really?" asked the son.

"Yes," the old woman answered.

Mother and son arrived at the king's palace. The king gave his daughter in marriage to the old woman's son. The wedding celebration lasted seven days and seven nights. There was merriment and feasting until the revelers fell down.

After the wedding, the old woman's son brought the king's daughter to his palace, where we will leave them while we turn our attention to Beardless.

The beardless sorcerer knew about everything and decided to take the magic ring away from the king's son.

He bought some multi-colored beads, coral, pearls, and various crystal knick-knacks, and he set out for the palace of the king's son. He opened a small shop in front of the palace and began selling his wares.

Every day the wife of the king's son sent her guard to the shop to buy beads and coral. She looked out the window at Beardless's shop and thought, "If I went there myself, I could pick out the best items."

One day she did just that. Beardless was very happy. "What do you want, My Lady?" he asked.

The wife of the king's son selected some coral beads and asked, "How much do they cost?"

"My lady," said Beardless, "I won't sell those coral beads for money."

"Then what do you want?"

"Rusty old rings. I don't need money."

"All right," said the wife of the king's son. "It just so happens that we have a rusty ring at the palace. I'll bring it right away."

She got the ring and gave it to Beardless. Then she took the coral beads and went home.

Now Beardless had the magic ring. He almost went mad with happiness. In the blink of an eye, he placed the ring on his finger, and the Arabs appeared.

"What do you want, Beardless?" asked the Arabs.

"Bring the king's son and the old woman here to my shop. And take me and the wife of the king's son to an island in the middle of the sea. Transport the new palace there, too."

This was not difficult for the Arabs to do. In a flash they had transported the palace of the king's son to an island in the middle of the sea. Then they transported Beardless and the wife of the king's son to the palace. The king's son and the old woman were transported to Beardless's shop.

The king's son opened his eyes and saw that he was sitting with the old woman in Beardless's shop and that the king's daughter was nowhere to be seen. He understood immediately what had happened. He grieved and wept, but it could not be helped.

"Mother," said the king's son. "Life has no value to me. Stay here, and I'll wander the earth. Perhaps I'll be able to take revenge on Beardless. If I return safe and sound, I'll be your son and you'll be my mother. If I don't return, may God watch over you."

The king's son equipped himself for the journey. He kissed the old woman's hand, grabbed his cat, and set out. He traveled for a day, two days, three day, four days—in short, he traveled for an entire week.

Finally, he came to a village. It was growing dark. He entered the village and knocked at someone's gate. The master of the house opened the gate.

"Who are you?" asked the master of the house. "Where are you going so late at night?"

"I am a traveler," said the king's son. "Please let me spend the night with you. I'll leave at the crack of dawn."

"Why not?" asked the master of the house, and he let the king's son come into the house. "A guest is always sent by God." He invited the young man to sit down on his bed, and he gave him something to eat. Then the master of the house took a seat and grabbed a club. He gave the club to his guest.

The king's son was surprised by his behavior. "What is this club for?" he asked.

"Have patience," said the master of the house. "You'll soon find out."

The king's son had barely begun to eat when enormous mice came running from all directions and attacked the food. The king's son and the master of the house began beating them with clubs in order to save the food. With one hand they beat off the mice, and with the other hand they grabbed the food.

When he understood the situation, the king's son jumped up from his seat and untied his leather sack. The cat jumped out of the leather sack and rushed after the mice. The mice ran off in all directions.

The master of the house was amazed. So this was the kind of guest he had! Even the mice feared him.

It turned out that there wasn't a single cat in this country. The king's son lived for several days with the people of that land. His hosts ate and drank in peace. The cat scared the mice so badly that it was as if they had all disappeared.

Life had become unbearable for the mice. They organized a protest and went to their king with their complaint. "The son of a certain king has appeared in our country, and he brought along a cat. We are seized with such terror that we dare not go out of our holes. Look at us. We are dying of hunger."

The King of the Mice selected the bravest mouse and ordered him to go to the king's son. "Go to the king's son and say, 'Ask for anything you wish, but take your cat and go far away from here.'"

The brave mouse approached the king's son. "Hello, King's Son," said the mouse. "The King of the Mice has ordered me to say, 'Ask for anything you wish, but take your cat and leave our country!'"

"There is a palace on an island in the sea," the king's son answered. "Beardless lives in that palace, and he has my rusty ring. If you can get my ring away from him, I will take my cat and leave. If you can't get the ring, I will stay here."

The brave mouse ran to tell the King of the Mice that Beardless was living in a palace on an island in the middle of the sea, and that he had a ring, and that as long as that ring wasn't brought to the king's son, the lad would not leave.

After the King of the Mice heard this information, he sent the bravest mouse to Beardless's palace to steal the ring and bring it to the king's son.

The brave mouse set out for Beardless's palace. The mouse dug a road beneath the sea. She swam for a day and dug for a day. After a week had passed, she reached the palace. That night she dug a hole and got into the palace, where she saw Beardless sleeping.

Every evening when Beardless went to bed, he placed the magic ring under his tongue so that the wife of the king's son wouldn't steal it, place it on her finger, and ask the Arabs to help her.

The mouse ran hither, thither, and yon, but she couldn't find the ring. Then she looked in Beardless's mouth and saw the ring. The mouse looked in the pantry and saw a bottle of vinegar and a pepper cellar filled with black pepper. The mouse dipped her tail first into the vinegar and then into the pepper. Then she stuck her tail into Beardless's nose. Beardless sneezed, and the ring fell out of his mouth. It was just what the mouse was waiting for. She grabbed the ring and headed home.

The mice brought the ring to the king's son, who took his cat and left the country, just as he had promised.

After coming to an open space, the young man put on the ring. The Arabs appeared immediately. "What is your command, King's Son?" they asked.

"Take me back to my country."

The Arabs carried the king's son back to his country.

Then the king's son said, "Go to the island in the middle of the sea and drag Beardless out of the palace. Throw him into the sea. Then transport the palace with all its furnishings and the king's daughter to its former place."

When the king's son saw his wife, he was so happy that he didn't know what to do. They sat and conversed and told one another about everything that had happened to them. The old woman rejoiced in their good fortune.

They lived as man and wife in love and harmony until the day they died. They had to wait for their happiness, but it finally came, just as your happiness, too, will come to you.

Arisa is a dish prepared with chicken and wheat.

THE PEASANT'S SON AND THE KING'S DAUGHTER

*T*here once lived a peasant who had nothing on earth except his wife and children. One day he threw a shovel over his shoulder and set out to work in the field.

When he came to the field, he saw two snakes grappling there. One snake was so beautiful and white that one couldn't take one's eyes off it. The other snake was so horrible and black that it made one sick to one's stomach to look at it.

The peasant saw that the horrible-looking snake was on the verge of tearing apart the beautiful snake. The peasant struck the black snake on the head and killed it on the spot.

The white snake crawled up to the peasant and said, "You have saved the life of the daughter of the King of the Snakes. Come with me to my father. If he asks what you want for a reward for rescuing me, say, 'I need nothing. Just give me a fez, a fife, and a tobacco pouch.' "

The peasant followed the snake. They went on until they came to a large snake hole.

"Wait until I return," said the snake, and she disappeared down the hole.

The peasant waited one, two, three hours. Suddenly, an enormous, handsome snake came crawling out of the hole.

After crawling out of the hole, the snake bowed to the peasant and said, "Thank you, brother, for saving my daughter from the black snake. Ask for anything you want as a reward."

"I need nothing," said the peasant. "Just give me a fez, a fife, and a tobacco pouch."

The King of the Snakes crawled back into the hole and brought out what the peasant had asked for.

The peasant went back to water the field. Toward evening, he went home. There was an old trunk in the house. He hid the fez, fife, and tobacco pouch in the trunk. "Let them lie there," he thought. "One day they may be of use."

After some time had passed, the peasant became ill. He took to his bed and soon died. He left behind his wife and son.

The son grew up to be a clever lad. One day he said, "Listen, Mother, how long must we toil and suffer like this? I'm going to go to a foreign land where I can earn a little money."

"You know best, Son," said his mother. "If that is your plan, go ahead and do what you want."

The young man prepared for the journey. "Mother, do you have some sort of fez that I can wear?" he asked. "Maybe I can use it to scoop some water from a stream when I get thirsty."

"When you were little, your father brought a fez home. God only knows where it is now. I'll look for it."

The young man's mother searched and searched. She looked in the old trunk and found the fez. Happy, she gave it to her son.

The boy bid his mother farewell and left home. He pulled the fez down over his head and set out. Whether he traveled for a long or short time, only God knows. Finally, he spied a spring and decided to stop.

He sat down, spread out his tablecloth, and began eating. Suddenly, he noticed that not far away some thieves were sitting and that they, too, were eating. A pile of loot lay beside them.

They noticed the young man and called him over. "Hey, boy, gather some brushwood and throw it on the fire."

The peasant's son put on the fez and gathered some dry twigs. He threw part of them onto the fire and put part of the twigs by the thieves' side. Then he took off the fez to scratch his head.

"Hey, boy," the thieves shouted, "we told you to gather some brushwood. Why are you malingering?"

The peasant's son understood right away what had happened. "This isn't an ordinary fez if they didn't see me," he thought.

"See how much brushwood I brought you," he said to the thieves.

"When did you manage to do that? All right, now take off."

The young man went aside and put on the fez. He became invisible. Then he approached the thieves. The thieves had spread out their stolen loot and money and were dividing it up. The young man didn't lose his head. He grabbed fistful after fistful of money.

The thieves saw that the amount of money was decreasing. They began shouting and quarrelling about who had taken it. Finally, they came to blows.

The peasant's son crammed his tobacco pouch to overflowing with money and took off. Whether he traveled a long or short time, only God knows. Finally, he came to a country where he decided to work to earn some money.

He rented a small shop and began trading. He sold everything at half price to lure in shoppers. To get goods for his shop, he put on the fez of invisibility and went to the shops of the rich merchants who had earned ill-gotten gains by cheating people. He grabbed their wares and brought them to his shop, where he sold everything very reasonably.

Life became unbearable for the merchants of that country. They assembled and went to the king with their complaint. "Take pity on us. We have become impoverished. We can't maintain our wives in style, and all because of the newcomer. It's as if the devil himself takes our wares away in broad daylight. Shoppers don't come to us because the newcomer practically gives away his wares. For the love of God, help us. If you don't, we'll have to leave the country."

The king's daughter turned to the merchants and said, "Don't be sad. I'll get to the bottom of this mystery. I'll find out what the stranger is up to."

The king's daughter ordered that the best wine be brought to her. She ordered that a sheep be cooked and that a turkey be roasted. She ordered that many more dishes be prepared. Then she set out for the peasant's shop.

She entered the shop and said, "Hello, friend! You have been trading in our town for a long time. Yet you haven't come to me even once. I have been waiting and watching for you until I've worn out my eyes with watching."

When the peasant's son heard these words, he was so happy that he lost his head. With the food the king's daughter had brought, he entertained her royally. They ate and drank and conversed as they feasted. The king's daughter kept pouring wine until the peasant's son grew tipsy.

She tried to find out about him. "See how I love you," she said. "I came to you on my own, but you won't tell me how it is that you've gotten wealthy by selling your wares cheaply."

The young man was drunk, so he told the king's daughter that his magic fez had helped him. After telling her his secret, he fell asleep.

That was just what the king's daughter was waiting for. She grabbed the fez and went back to the palace. The merchants brought gifts to the king's daughter in gratitude for her saving them from ruin.

Meanwhile, the peasant's son awoke and began looking for his fez. It was nowhere to be found. He was sad, but nothing could be done. He gathered his wares, lifted them onto his back, and set out for his native land.

Whether he traveled for a long or short time, only God knows. He walked on for one, two, three days—in short, for an entire week. Finally, he came to his country.

He was happy to be home. And his poor mother was overjoyed to see him. He lived with his mother until the money was spent.

When only a few coins remained, he gave part of them to his mother for small household expenses. He kept a fifty-*dram** coin for himself. He put it into his father's tobacco pouch. He put the pouch in his pocket and set out for the country where the king's daughter had duped him so craftily.

Whether he traveled a long or short time, only God knows. Eventually, he came to a village. "I'll stop here," he thought, "and I'll change this coin into small change so that I can buy something to eat."

He took the tobacco pouch out of his pocket and untied it. To his surprise, instead of a fifty-*dram* coin, he found a hundred-*dram* coin in the tobacco pouch. He understood right away what had happened. "Apparently, this is a magic tobacco pouch," he thought.

He didn't touch the money. He put it back in the pouch and continued on his journey. Finally, he came to the country where he had rented a shop. He went back to the same place, rented a new shop, and began selling his wares again.

Several days passed, and the merchants went to the king's daughter once again. "For the love of God, save us from the lad. He is ruining us again."

The king's daughter took an herb that would make the peasant go to sleep and set out for the young man's shop. She entered and greeted him as she had done the first time. Once again, she asked what his secret was. In the simplicity of his soul, the peasant's son told her again.

The king's daughter gave him a potion with the herb in it to drink. The young man went to sleep immediately. He slept so deeply that he wouldn't have heard anything, even if someone began dragging him by the legs. That is just what the king's daughter wanted. She took the tobacco pouch and went back to the palace.

Again the merchants went to the king's daughter with gifts in gratitude for her saving them from ruin.

The peasant's son slept one, two hours, one, two days, and then he finally awoke. There was no tobacco pouch and no money to be seen.

Once again he set out for his own country. "All right," he thought, "just you wait, King's Daughter. I'll play such a trick on you that you'll remember it forever. My fife will help me."

He traveled on until he reached his own country. After arriving home, he said to his mother, "Be patient a little longer. Soon I'll return home for good. Forgive me for having to leave just one more time."

He took the fife, kissed his mother, and set out on his journey. Whether he traveled for a long or short time, only God knows. Finally, he came to a mountain and said, "I think I'll play the fife. It may be enchanted."

He began blowing, and suddenly an army appeared in the valley. The army was so enormous that the end was not in sight.

"I think I'll blow on the other end," he thought. He had barely started to blow when the entire army disappeared in the flash of an eye.

"Fine," thought the young man. "With this fife I can deal with the king's daughter."

He hurried to the country where the king's daughter lived. Whether he traveled for a long or short time, only God knows, but eventually he reached her country.

He stood in the middle of a field, directed the fife at the king's palace, and began playing. In an instant an immense army appeared from out of nowhere, and it was ten times greater than the king's army.

The king and his nazirs, or officials, and viziers, or ministers of state, took fright. "Where did that army come from? What will happen now?"

"Never fear," said the king's daughter. "These are the antics of the peasant's son. I'll go to him and find out what's going on."

The king's daughter got ready and left. She walked on until she found the peasant's son. Again they ate and drank and feasted. Once again she gave the young man too much to drink, and he told her everything. "My magic is in this fife," he said. "When you blow in one end, an army will appear. When you blow in the other end, it disappears."

The king's daughter was so happy that she couldn't feel the legs beneath her. She gave the young man a sleeping potion, took the fife, and went home. After arriving at the palace, she blew in the other end of the fife, and the army disappeared, as if it had never existed.

The king gave his daughter new clothes as a reward. He dressed her from head to toe in finery.

Meanwhile, the peasant's son slept soundly for a couple of days. When he awoke, he saw that his fife was gone and that the king's daughter was gone. He understood that the king's daughter had duped him for the third time. "Just you wait, King's Daughter," he thought. "You'll dance to the tune of my pipe yet."

After grieving, the young man set out for another land. "I'll earn a little money," he thought. "Then I'll return to my country and light a fire in my own hearth."

While thinking, he walked on. Whether he traveled a long or short time, only God knows. Finally, he reached the sea and walked along the seashore.

He was thirsty. On the slope of a small mountain sprawled an enormous garden, which was full of white and red grapes. "How nice," the peasant's son thought. "I'll eat some grapes. They will quench my thirst, and then I'll take a stroll in the garden."

He entered the garden and plucked a bunch of red grapes. After eating a few, he immediately turned into an enormous buffalo. He grieved, but nothing could be done.

Down on his luck, he went up to the white grapes. He ate a few and turned back into a human being. "How nice," he thought. "Now I know what to do."

He picked two baskets full of grapes, one red and the other white. Then he set out to visit the king's daughter. Whether he traveled a long or short time, only God knows, but finally he reached the country where the king's daughter lived.

He hid the basket of white grapes in an unnoticeable place. Then he hoisted the basket of red grapes onto his shoulders and went right to the king's palace.

He stood in front of the windows of the palace and cried, "Who wants some grapes? Take what I have left."

The king's daughter looked out the window and saw the grape vendor. She sent her servants to him.

"Go, buy all of the grapes," she said.

The servants bought the grapes. As soon as the king's daughter put a single grape into her mouth, she turned into a huge, black buffalo. She walked swaying from side to side, like a buffalo.

The king summoned all the doctors in the country, but not one of them could help his daughter.

The peasant's son went to the king and said, "Your Majesty, I can cure your daughter."

"I feel sorry for you, son" said the king. "You are still young. You'd do better to leave. Even the best doctors in the world couldn't cure my daughter. How could you?"

"If I don't succeed in curing her, punish me," said the peasant's son.

The young man was led to the chambers of the king's daughter. He took with him some white grapes and a sturdy whip.

He entered the chambers of the king's daughter and began to whip her. While he was whipping her, he said, "Tell me where you have hidden the fez, the tobacco pouch, and the fife. If you don't tell me, I'll whip you all the more."

The buffalo fell at the young man's feet and begged, "For God's sake, save me, and I'll bring everything to you."

"No," said the peasant's son. "First bring me my things, and then I'll heal you so that once again you'll be as you were."

The king's daughter in the body of a buffalo led the young man to the place where the fez, the tobacco pouch, and the fife were hidden.

The peasant's son was happy. He put the magic objects into his pocket. Only then did he place the basket of white grapes before the buffalo.

The buffalo rushed at the white grapes. In an instant she ate all of them and turned into a girl again. She was so beautiful that no pen could describe her beauty.

The king was informed that his daughter had been healed. Rejoicing, he went to his daughter, kissed her on the forehead, and embraced the peasant's son.

"Listen son," said the king. "I don't have an heir. Marry my daughter. After my death, you will become king and you will rule my kingdom."

The peasant's son was happy. He sent the king's servants to fetch his mother.

After she arrived, the wedding of the peasant's son and the king's daughter was celebrated for seven days and seven nights. The guests made merry and feasted so heartily that they were exhausted.

The king's daughter and the peasant attained their happiness. May you attain your happiness, too.

---

*The *dram* is the basic monetary unit in Armenia.

DZHEIRAN-OGLY,*
THE DEER'S SON

*T*here once lived a poor man who had nothing to eat. One day he said to his wife, "Wife, let's go to another town. Perhaps it will be better there."

They set out and went to the city of King Turtamb. The town was surrounded with a wall that had two gates—an entrance and an exit. As they approached the entrance, the man's wife went into labor. The guard wouldn't let the couple into town, so the poor woman lay on the ground while her son was being born.

That night King Turtamb dreamed that outside the city gates a woman had given birth to a son who would chop off the king's head when he grew up. The king summoned his guard and ordered, "Walk around the city wall. If you see a newborn child, bring the child here."

One of the guards went out the gate and saw a poorly dressed woman lying on the ground, clutching a newborn to her breast. The newborn was swaddled in rags, and an old man with a pipe in his hand stood beside them.

"Let's go, little uncle, the king wants to see you," said the guard.

"What business do I have with the king, brother? I am a poor man. And as you can see, my wife has just given birth to a son."

"Don't waste time talking. Just come along."

They went to the king and bowed low seven times. After the eighth bow, they shook hands and stood at attention.

"Old man, is this woman your wife?"

"Yes, she is your Majesty's obedient servant."

"Is the child a boy or a girl?"

"A boy, your Majesty."

"How much would you take for the child?"

"You want me to sell you the child?"

"Sell him. Your wife will give birth to another child."

"Listen to the king, brother," advised the nazir, the king's official. "Ask for 300 pieces of gold, and from now on you'll live like a human being. You'll stop hiccupping from hunger."

"You know best, King Turtamb," said the poor man.

"How much do you want?"

"As much as you want to give me."

"Nazir, give this man as much gold as his baby weighs. Then tell him to leave," said the king.

The baby was weighed. After the poor man received the gold, he left.

"Take the baby and go to the mountains. Kill him there. Wet his diapers with his blood and bring them to me," the king said to his nazir.

The nazir set out for the mountains with the child. On the way, he thought, "What has come into the king's head that he imagines this child will grow up and chop off his head? It would be better for me to shoot a bird, wet the diapers with its blood, and take them to the king.

The nazir placed the baby under a bush. Then he shot a bird and covered the diapers in its blood. He took the diapers to the king.

The baby lay beneath the bush, crying loudly. A doe heard his cry and came to him. She gave him her milk.

Thus three years passed. The little boy was raised in a herd of deer and followed the doe, his benefactress, around. When he was almost nine years old, he met King Turtamb's son, who was hunting in the forest.

The king's son was amazed. Could a doe have given birth to a little boy?

That evening, after arriving home, the king's son asked his father, "Father, have you ever known a doe to give birth to a boy?"

"No, Son, that couldn't be. You must have imagined it."

"No, I didn't imagine it. Let's go hunting together tomorrow, and you'll see with your own eyes."

The next day father and son mounted their horses and went to the mountains. The king's son galloped ahead and frightened the deer. The boy, whose name was Dzheiran-ogly, which means the Deer's Son, was with the herd of deer.

King Turtamb looked at the boy and was amazed. The boy, who had been raised on deer milk, was strong as a buffalo.

"Just wait. I'll order three rows of chains to be stretched out, and the boy will be caught," said the king.

The king wasted much money on the making of three rows of chains. Dzheiran-ogly ran up to the chains and instantly tore them apart. He broke free and rushed after the doe who was his benefactress. The king didn't know what to do.

"King Turtamb," said the nazir, "I know an old man who is 150 years old. Let's call him and see what he advises."

The old man was summoned. "Grandfather," said the king, "there is a boy in our region who was raised by a doe. We can't catch him. Tell us what to do."

"Your Majesty, when I was nazir during your father's reign, there was a similar case. Strings were ordered from Ispagan,** and the person was caught with these strings."

The king sent emissaries to Ispagan. They brought back the strings and secured them on all sides of the mountain. Then the horsemen set out to poison the deer.

When he saw that the deer were being harmed, Dzheiran-ogly came running and rushed at the strings. He hit them with all his might. He wanted to tear them apart, but he couldn't. He roared so that the mountains and ravines resounded with his cry. The king's servants came running and caught him. They tied him up with the strings and led him away. The doe wept bitterly, following the boy with her eyes.

Dzheiran-ogly was brought to court and placed with his peers to learn to speak. Within ten days, the lad was speaking.

The king was happy. He decided that the boy would grasp learning easily and sent him to school.

One day the king's son wanted to find out how much money and possessions his father had. One after another, he opened thirty-five rooms and saw that there was a great deal of wealth. The guard wouldn't let the king's son open the door to the fortieth room.

The young man got angry and struck the guard's face. "Son of a dog, how dare you prevent me from looking at my father's treasure?"

He pushed the guard aside and opened the door. The portrait of an indescribable beauty wearing her hair in forty braids was hanging on the wall of the room. The king's son fell to the floor in a faint.

His mother and father learned what had happened. They came running and sprinkled water on him until the king's son came to.

"What is wrong with you, Son?" they asked.

"It would be better for me to have died than to live without the Maiden with Forty Braids. Whatever comes of it, I must go after her."

Dzheiran-ogly came and saw that everyone had gathered around the king's son. "What's going on?" he asked.

"The king's son has seen the portrait of the Maiden with Forty Braids, and he wants to go after her," they answered.

"That's not your worry. I'll go and fetch her," Dzheiran-ogly said to the king's son.

The king's son arose and gave Dzheiran-ogly a slap for talking in that manner.

Dzheiran-ogly grabbed the king's son, raised him up, and said, "If you try that again, I'll throw you to the ground, and you'll turn to dust."

"Lad, remember that he is your brother," said King Turtamb.

The next morning the king's son and Dzheiran-ogly mounted their horses and set out.

"I was wrong to strike Dzheiran-ogly," thought the king's son. "He will be useful to me on the way. He'll take care of my horse and serve me."

Whether they traveled a long or short time, only God knows. On the journey, Dzheiran-ogly said, "Don't be frightened if we meet a giant called a *dev*."***

"People aren't afraid of *devs*. Why should I be afraid?" asked the king's son.

They went on and crossed many mountains. Suddenly, they met a giant. The king's son bit his lip so hard out of fear that blood flowed.

"Hey, lad, what's wrong?" asked Dzheiran-ogly.

"What kind of monster is that?"

"I said you'd be frightened. Let's go. Don't be afraid."

"Hey, folks, who are you?" asked the *dev*.

"We've come to visit you," said Dzheiran-ogly.

"Please do. I was roaming the mountains searching for human beings, but you have come of your own free will. It's been a long time since I've eaten human flesh. I've missed it."

"It's early to be boasting, brother."

They hurried on and entered the monster's cave. A lame *dev* was standing by the kettle. He was stirring soup with an enormous spoon.

"Give me the scoop," said Dzheiran-ogly, "and I'll test the soup to see if it's salty enough."

The *dev* struck him with the hot handle of the scoop. "Don't stick your nose in my business," said the *dev*.

Dzheiran-ogly tore the scoop from his hands and struck him with the handle.

"Ooh, brothers, he broke my hand," cried the *dev*.

Dzheiran-ogly scooped up some soup. He tasted it and began tucking in.

"Leave a bit for us, brothers," said the *dev*.

The main *dev* spoke to Dzheiran-ogly. "Help me bring a big rock here from the road."

They approached the rock. "Well, let's give it a try. Lift it up," said Dzheiran-ogly.

"There are seven of us, and together we can't lift it," said the *dev*. "We rolled it down from the mountain with great difficulty."

"Well, grab hold, and we'll see," said Dzheiran-ogly.

The *dev* bent over and wanted to lift the rock, but he grew weak and began shaking.

"Step aside," said Dzheiran-ogly. He lifted the rock and threw it over the mountain.

After observing this act, the *dev* was terrified. His hair stood on end. He went up to his brothers and said, "We're in trouble, brothers. That is either Dzheiran-ogly or another hero. We must ask him."

The *dev* turned to Dzheiran-ogly. "Brother guest, I hope you won't take offense if I ask whether you are Dzheiran-ogly."

"Yes, I am Dzheiran-ogly. How do you know me?"

"The day you were born, the mountains and ravines howled, 'Dzheiran-ogly has appeared.' When I heard it then, I shook in my boots. I know you have come to get my sister, the Maiden with Forty Braids, Dzheiran-ogly. Take her. You have my permission."

As soon as the sun shone in the ravine, the *devs* and Dzheiran-ogly set out hunting. The seven *devs* went in one direction, and Dzheiran-ogly went in the other direction. The king's son stayed in the cave with his bride-to-be, the *dev*'s sister, the Maiden with Forty Braids.

The king's son and the Maiden with Forty Braids began preparing dinner. The king's son poured water into the kettle and lit the fire. He cut up some meat and threw it into the kettle.

While the meal was cooking, the Maiden with Forty Braids said, "Sit down, King's son. I'll sleep for a while in your lap."

The king's son sat down, and the maiden placed her head in his lap and fell asleep. The young man played with her braids and noticed three keys in them. He put his cloak beneath her head and got up. He decided to open the locked rooms, whose doors the keys opened. He opened one door and a second door, but the rooms were empty. He opened a third door and saw the White Dev attached to a chain. There were two kettles in front of him. One was filled with pilaf and mutton, and the other was filled with water. The White Dev was looking at the kettles and straining on the chain that held him, but he couldn't reach the kettles.

"You came in the nick of time," cried the White Dev. "Give me two scoops of pilaf. These unscrupulous people have kept me chained for forty days without feeding me."

The king's son gave the *dev* ten scoops of pilaf.

"Give me another scoop of pilaf, brother, just one more," begged the *dev* until he had eaten the entire kettle of pilaf.

"Now give me some water to drink," begged the *dev*.

"I can't lift the kettle," said the king's son.

"Fasten the chain to the kettle and give it to me."

The king's son fastened the chain to the kettle and gave it to the *dev*. The *dev* took the chain in his mouth and began pulling the kettle. He drew the kettle to himself and drank up all the water.

As soon as he had drunk all the water, he acquired his former strength. He tore apart his chains and with one end of the chain struck the forehead of the king's son. The young man lost consciousness and fell. After piling hay on his body, the White Dev grabbed the Maiden with Forty Braids and dashed home.

The *devs* returned in the evening carrying what they had bagged on their hunt. Later, Dzheiran-ogly came carrying what he had bagged, which was twice as much as what the *devs* had bagged.

The *devs* entered their home and asked, "Where is our sister?"

"And where is my brother?" asked Dzheiran-ogly. He grabbed the scoop and hit the *devs*, one after the other, on the head. "Bring me my brother," he ordered.

The *devs* found the king's son lying in the hay groaning. They gave him a kick, and he got up. "What happened to you, lad?"

"Brothers, the White Dev was chained here. I went into the room and gave him some pilaf to eat and some water to drink. He tore apart the chains, and I don't remember what happened after that."

"Aye-aye-aye," said the *devs*. "Your brother has released our nephew. We aren't to blame. He wanted to kidnap our sister. We caught him and chained him to the wall. Now he has broken the chains and taken our sister."

"I'm leaving my brother with you as security, and I'm going to fetch your sister," said Dzheiran-ogly. "If upon my return I notice that you have abused my brother, I'll chop off your heads." Having uttered these words, Dzheiran-ogly jumped on his horse and galloped away.

"He won't come back," said the *devs*. "Now we'll deal with his brother."

They chained the king's son to a post and put a lamp on his head. Meanwhile, Dzheiran-ogly reached the White Dev's home. He went in and saw the Maiden with Forty Braids sitting there.

"Maiden, how did you get here?" asked Dzheiran-ogly.

"Not of my own free will. I'm here because of what your brother did."

Shortly thereafter, the White Dev stuck his head in the door and saw that Dzheiran-ogly was sitting beside the maiden. "This is bad business," he thought.

"Come in, come in," said Dzheiran-ogly.

But how could the White Dev enter when his legs wouldn't obey him? Instead, Dzheiran-ogly came out of the house and went into the yard. The White Dev began running, but Dzheiran-ogly chased him. He cut off the White Dev's head, put the Maiden with Forty Braids on his horse, and galloped away.

When he reached the *devs'* cave, he left the maiden in the yard and entered. He saw his brother standing there white as chalk.

"Rescue me, brother," said the king's son.

When Dzheiran-ogly saw what the *devs* had done to his brother, he grabbed his sword and cut off five heads. The remaining two *devs* fell to their knees before him. "For God's sake, spare us," they begged.

"Look lively," said Dzheiran-ogly. "Equip us for a journey. We're setting out for home in the morning."

As soon as it was light, Dzheiran-ogly placed the fiancée of the king's son on the saddle and then mounted himself. He and the king's son set out.

When their journey was half over, they met a shepherd. They gave the shepherd some money and sent him ahead to give the king the news that his sons were on their way home with the fiancée.

When King Turtamb heard the news, he became thoughtful. By now he understood that the boy he had dreamed about so many years ago was none other than Dzheiran-ogly. He summoned his nazir and asked, "Do you think that I gave you the boy all those years ago so that you could keep him alive?"

"Your Majesty, I couldn't kill him in full conscience. I left the boy in the forest thinking that a wolf would eat him up or that he would cry himself to death."

"Executioner!" cried the king. "Chop off the nazir's head. He disobeyed my command." The executioner did as the king ordered.

To free himself of Dzheiran-ogly, the king decided to send the lad a horse that would bring him misfortune.

Meanwhile, Dzheiran-ogly said to his brother, "Let's rest beside this stream for a while. After news comes from town, we'll press on."

Dzheiran-ogly lay down beneath a willow. Three doves flew up to the tree and roosted on its branches. "I pity Dzheiran-ogly," said one of the doves.

"Why?" asked the other dove.

"Today King Turtamb is sending him a horse. When he attempts to mount it, he'll burn up."

"And if he doesn't mount it?"

"Then he'll be immured in a room where Shakhmar the Snake lives. The king will deceive Dzheiran-ogly. He'll say that he gave a promise to take him to the best room in the castle if he brought back the fiancée. Shakhmar the Snake will come slithering along and bite Dzheiran-ogly. Dzheiran-ogly will grab his sword and will cut off Shakhmar's head. Two drops of snake's blood will fall on Dzheiran-ogly, and he'll turn to stone." After uttering these words, the doves gave a coo and flew away.

Dzheiran-ogly collected himself. "Ah, ha! Who is going to rescue me?" he asked.

He saw the king's grooms coming toward him with a horse. They led the horse to him and said, "The king sent you this horse as a gift. Mount it and go to him."

"You mount it first. I want to see if the horse is a restive one."

"I wasn't ordered to do so."

"Mount, or I'll chop off your head!"

The groom mounted the horse and burned up in flames before Dzheiran-ogly's eyes.

The king's messenger informed His Majesty that Dzheiran-ogly had refused to mount the horse.

"That's all right," said King Turtamb. "Something even better is in store for him."

Dzheiran-ogly, the king's son, and the Maiden with Forty Braids arrived at court and stood before the king. The king was very happy indeed to see his son and his son's fiancée. But thoughts of revenge boiled in Dzheiran-ogly's heart.

The queen came to them. She kissed Dzheiran-ogly first and then her son and his fiancée.

"You know what, Son," the king said to Dzheiran-ogly, "I promised myself that if you returned safe and unharmed, I would give you the best room in the palace and you would spend the day in it. Go ahead and enter the room."

After Dzheiran-ogly entered the room, the king's servants immediately slammed the door behind him.

"Oh, oh," he sighed, "my end has come."

Not once in the past had he been afraid in difficult situations, but this time he was scared. He took out his sword and sat beside a stone wall. Beautiful Shakhmar the Snake stuck his head out of a chink and crawled up to Dzheiran-ogly. Shakhmar attacked Dzheiran-ogly. Dzheiran-ogly waved his sword and cut off Shakhmar's head. However, two drops of blood fell onto Dzheiran-ogly, and he turned to stone.

Years passed, and the king's son and the Maiden with Forty Braids had two sons. The king's wife and son told the Maiden with Forty Braids that long ago the king had seen in a dream that Dzheiran-ogly would cut off his head, so the king had him shut up in a room where Dzheiran-ogly had turned to stone because of the snake's blood.

"Bring me the keys, and I'll go take a look," said the Maiden with Forty Braids.

The king's son brought his wife the keys, and she hid them. She went into the room and sat beside the stone. She wept and told the walls what her mother-in-law and husband had told her. Then she left. She did so many times.

One day she came again and wept so much that she grew tired and fell asleep. That night she had a dream. A voice commanded, "Kill your two sons and wet the stone with their blood. If you do so, it will be all the better for your sons and for this man who has turned to stone."

The Maiden with Forty Braids killed her sons just as she had been ordered in the dream. She put her sons' blood on the stone, and suddenly both her sons and Dzheiran-ogly came alive. They embraced.

"Little sister, I will remember your kindness forever," said Dzheiran-ogly.

Then he drew his sword and went to the king. King Turtamb was listening to a man who had come to him to lodge a complaint and to ask for his help. When the king caught sight of Dzheiran-ogly, he trembled with every fiber of his being, and he lost heart.

Dzheiran-ogly bowed to the king and said, "Dismiss the man lodging a complaint! Today you must listen to my complaint."

The king ordered that the man lodging a complaint be ushered out.

"Your Majesty, if someone had a new garden and a villain vandalized it, what would you do with him?"

"I would order that he be blinded."

"Nazir, record his words."

"Your Majesty, if someone built a church and while passing it you noticed that a villain was destroying it with a crowbar, what would you do?"

"I would order two wide boards to be brought. Then I would order that the villain be placed on the boards and chopped to pieces."

"Nazir, record his words, and bring two boards."

After the boards were brought, King Turtamb himself took off his clothes and lay on the boards.

Dzheiran-ogly said, "I will carry out your judgment with my own hands."

He waved his sword, grabbed the king by the foot, and chopped him into small pieces. Then he cut off his head. The chopped-up body was placed in a sack and buried.

Dzheiran-ogly put on King Turtamb's clothes and began ruling the kingdom.

News of what happened reached the Maiden with Forty Braids. She came running, bowed seven times before Dzheiran-ogly, crossed her hands on her chest, and said, "I beg you, don't do anything else. Let your judgment end here."

"I give everyone else his freedom. You may go," said Dzheiran-ogly.

Dzheiran-ogly brought order to the kingdom. He ordered that his mother and father be brought to court. He went to the mountains and called the doe that had raised him. She came running and licked his hands and face. He kissed the doe and led her to the palace. Thereafter, he frequently slept with his head on the doe's chest.

They attained their heart's desire. May you attain yours, too.

Three apples fell from heaven—one for the storyteller and two for the listeners.

---

*Pronounced Zeerán-oogly.

**Also spelled Isfagan and Isfahan, Ispagan was a large city in Persia, present-day Iran.

***The *dev* is variously interpreted to be a monster, dragon, serpent, or giant. In Armenian mythology, *devs* are immortal spirits who inhabit old ruins. Some are good, such as Aralez, who licks the wounds of warriors fallen in battle. Others, such as the dragon Vishap, are evil.

THE EXTRAORDINARY CUCUMBER

*T*here once lived a gardener. One day an extraordinary cucumber, enormous as a barrel, was found growing in his garden. The gardener refused to sell the cucumber to anyone because he admired it so.

The king's son heard about the unusual cucumber. "I think I'll try to buy the cucumber," he thought. "The gardener probably won't dare refuse me since I am the king's son."

He went to the gardener and demanded the cucumber while pouring gold coins out of a bag.

"All right," said the gardener. "You are the king's son. It is difficult to refuse you, and you have given me a princely sum. Take the cucumber, but watch out! When you leave the garden, don't look back. Go straight ahead until you reach that tall sycamore over there. Then you can rest."

The king's son took the cucumber and left. Suddenly, he heard the sound of the *zurna** and the jingle-jangle of several tambourines. Someone cried out, "Hey, look back, look back!" But the king's son walked on without turning around.

Only when he had reached the tall plane tree did he stop to rest. "I think I'll cut open the cucumber," he thought. "After all, everyone wanted and tried to get it, but I was the one who succeeded. I'll have a look and see what's inside the cucumber."

He took out his knife. He barely started cutting into the cucumber when it split in two on its own. A beautiful, shapely maiden with golden hair stepped out of the cucumber.

"Who are you, beautiful maiden?" exclaimed the king's son. He was so struck with her beauty that he added, "Will you please be my bride?"

"All right, I agree to marry you," the beautiful maiden replied.

"But I can't take my bride to the king's palace just like that," said the king's son. "No, that is not our custom. Climb up into the plane tree and wait for me. No one will touch you there. I'll return for you and will take you to the palace with the respect and honor due you. I'll take you to my father accompanied by the playing of the *zurna* and the *dhol*.**

The maiden agreed. The king's son helped her climb up into the plane tree. She hid in its thick foliage and waited.

After a great deal of (or perhaps just a little) time had passed, an old woman approached the plane tree. She saw a shadow reflected in a spring beneath the plane tree. She raised her head and began calling the girl. "Oh, *balik-dzhan*,*** climb down to me. Show yourself."

"No, I won't climb down, *nani-dzhan*.**** I'm afraid of you. I'm sitting here waiting for my fiancé. He is coming soon to get me."

"Move over, and I'll climb up and sit beside you," said the old woman. "We'll wait for him together."

"No," replied the maiden. "That isn't necessary."

"Oh, all right." The old woman smirked maliciously. But to herself she thought, "It would be better if I put a spell on her and then made myself look like her. Then I'd marry the king's son in her place."

The old woman began casting a spell, repeating it and waving her arms. She bewitched the girl and turned her into a bird. Then she made herself resemble the girl. She climbed onto a branch and waited.

Soon the king's son came for the maiden. He was accompanied by his friends and musicians. He took the sorceress, whom he mistook for the girl, from the tree.

Meanwhile, a little bird that was really the enchanted maiden kept twirling around him attempting to sit on his shoulder. He took the bird off his shoulder and gave it to his friend. The bird broke free and alighted on the shoulder of the king's son again. The young man caught the bird and gave it to another friend. Again the bird flew to his shoulder. Finally, the bird got on his nerves. The king's son grabbed the bird and twisted its head off. Then he threw the bird into the garden.

Later, a mulberry tree, tall and leafy, grew on the spot where the bird's head touched the earth.

"Why do I need that tree?" asked the garden's owner. "It is just obstructing the light."

The gardener began chopping down the tree. As he was chopping, a wood chip the size of a spoon flew into the yard of a poor woman. It turned into a beautifully decorated wooden spoon. The poor woman picked it up and placed it in the silverware drawer.

The next morning after the poor old woman had left the house, the spoon fell from the silverware drawer, struck the ground, and turned into a beautiful, golden-haired maiden.

The girl tidied up the old woman's room. She swept the yard and put everything in its place. She made *tanov aboor*, which is yogurt soup. Then she turned into a spoon again and hid in the silverware drawer.

The old woman came home and just couldn't understand what was going on. "What happened? Who tidied up the house? Who swept? Who made *tanov aboor*?"

She went to her neighbors and said, "Listen, and I'll tell you about the strange happenings at my house. Everything is cleaned and swept. Dinner is prepared. But who is doing it for me? That's what I can't understand."

One of her neighbors gave the following advice: "Why don't you hide and watch what goes on in your absence. Perhaps then you'll find out."

The next day the old woman hid behind the rug that hung on the wall. She peeked out and saw how the spoon fell out of the silverware drawer and turned into a beautiful maiden. She saw the girl tidying the house and putting everything in its place. She saw the girl kindle a fire in the *tonir****** to bake a flat bread called *lavash*.

After the girl had done everything, she wanted to scamper back into the silverware drawer. However, the old woman grabbed her by the hem of her skirt and wouldn't let go.

The little maiden begged, "Let me go *nani-dzhan*. I don't want to be a human being all the time. Let me go."

"No, I won't let you go," the old woman said. "I have a son. He'll come home soon, and he'll marry you."

"I can't marry your son, *nani-dzhan*. I'm betrothed to another man."

"Then be a daughter to me and a sister to my son," said the old woman.

"Very well," said the girl. "For the time being I'll live with you on the condition that you don't ask me any questions."

The golden-haired maiden began living with the old woman. But what about the king's son? He was living with his sorceress wife, and his life was joyless and melancholy.

After the passage of much time, or perhaps it was a little time, the king issued a decree. A horse from the king's stable was to be placed in every home to be fed and cared for.

A scraggly horse was led to the household of the old woman. "How can I take care of the king's horse?" she asked the king's servants. "I have no strength, and I have nothing to feed the horse."

"This horse belongs to the king's son," answered the servants. "Feed the horse however you wish. It's the king's decree."

When the beautiful maiden learned that the horse of the king's son had been brought to them, she said, "Don't worry, *nani-dzhan*, I'll look after the horse."

The maiden tied the sickly horse to a post in the yard and whispered to him, "My dear little horse, I'll rinse your hair in spring water. I'll pour water on your legs, and I'll plant grass in the earth. You'll eat the grass and get healthy."

Everything happened as she said. The horse began to recover. Its hair glistened, and its mane began to curl.

The day arrived when the king's horses were to be taken back to the royal stables. The girl went to the horse and said, "My dear horse, when the time comes to lead you away, lie down on the ground and remain there. However hard they beat you, don't get up."

The king's servants came, and the king's son came after his horse with them. The servants beat the horse and urged him on, but he lay there without budging.

"To what degree have you overfed this horse?" the king's son asked the old woman. "He won't budge from this spot."

"It wasn't me, but my daughter, who looked after the horse," the old woman answered.

"Then call your daughter. Let her manage the horse."

The maiden came when called and shouted to the horse, "Why aren't you getting up? Do you want to act fickle in front of your master? Apparently, your master is fickle, too. He doesn't know how to keep his word."

She had only to say these words, and the horse rose and set out for the king's palace. The king's son looked at her and saw that the beautiful maiden resembled the girl that came out of the cucumber much more than his wife did.

The king's son went back to the palace, but he lost the ability to sleep. He had no peace and lost his appetite, too. The next day he issued a decree that someone from every household had to come to court to comb wool.

The combers gathered at the palace, and the golden-haired maiden was among them. The women worked well. They finished the work in the allotted time.

The king's son went up to them and said, "Now tell me what each one of you wants to receive as a reward."

One woman asked for a shawl. Another asked for beads, and yet another wanted a bracelet.

When the golden-haired maiden's turn came, she said, "Give me a ripe pomegranate, a little doll, and a sharp razor."

The king's son was surprised by her strange request. Nevertheless, he brought everything she asked for.

After receiving her gift, the maiden set out down a deserted mountain road. She turned off the road and hid behind a dog rose bush, which is a European wild rose bush.

The king's son followed the girl and hid on the other side of the bush.

The girl sat down beneath the bush and said, "Oh, pomegranate, pomegranate, listen while I tell you about my sorrow. My sorrow is so great that it will make you split and break to pieces. Listen, doll, and I'll tell you about my sorrow. Then you must dance for me. Listen, razor, and I'll tell you about my sorrow, and then you must sharpen yourself as sharp as can be, razor."

The maiden began telling her tale. "I was placed under a spell and put in a cucumber. The king's son set me free and left me in a tree. A wicked sorceress found me and turned me into a bird. My fiancé, the king's son, tore off my head. I became a shady tree, but I was chopped down. Then I turned into a wooden spoon. When I came out of the spoon, I wasn't allowed to go back in . . . ."

As she was speaking, the pomegranate split open and broke into pieces. The doll began dancing, and the razor became sharper and sharper.

The maiden finished her tale and wanted to slit her throat with the razor. At that moment, the king's son ran up to her. After embracing her, he took her to the palace. When the king learned what had happened, he punished the sorceress. A splendid wedding was held for the king's son and his real bride.

They attained their heart's desire. May you attain your heart's desire, too.

---

*The *zurna* is a wooden wind instrument that sounds similar to the clarinet or bugle.

**Dhol* means "drum."

***Balik-dzhan* means "little child–dear soul."

****Nani-dzhan* means "mother–dear soul."

*****The *tonir* is a clay oven set in the ground.

PART 4

TALES OF EVERYDAY LIFE

THE GOOD DEED

A peasant's oxcart turned over on the road, and sheaves of wheat came tumbling out. The driver of the cart didn't know what to do.

But if God sends down disaster, He sends help shortly thereafter. At that very moment, the oxcart driver's neighbor was walking down the road. Of course, the neighbor helped the driver to load the sheaves of wheat onto the oxcart. Then the neighbor joined the driver on his journey. The neighbor hopped into the cart, and the two men continued on their way.

"You were lucky," the neighbor told the oxcart driver. "If I hadn't happened by, could you have lifted everything onto the oxcart alone?"

"Thank you very much," said the peasant. "I really couldn't have done it alone."

The driver and his neighbor continued their journey.

Soon the neighbor asked, "Well, how do you feel now, brother?" Then he added, "How nice it is that I happened on you and helped you load the cart!"

"Well, after all, what are neighbors for?" retorted the peasant.

The two men journeyed on in silence. Finally, the neighbor asked, "Why are you silent? After all, if I hadn't met up with you, you'd have been in a fix. You'd still be in need of help."

The neighbor kept conversing in this manner during the entire journey.

Understanding that his neighbor wasn't going to leave him in peace, finally the peasant shouted, "Who-o-a, oxen. Stop!"

After the oxen had come to a halt, the peasant overturned the cart himself. He threw the sheaves of wheat that he had been carrying in the cart all around on the ground.

Turning to his neighbor, the exasperated peasant shouted, "Now I'm free of you, brother. Why did you get tangled in my hair anyway? Go your own way. I won't ask you for help again, you can be sure of that!"

THE CUSTOMER AND
THE HATTER

A customer once went to a hatter with a piece of sheepskin. "Make me a hat from this piece of sheepskin," he commanded.

"All right," said the hatter. "I'll make you a hat."

After leaving the shop, the customer began thinking. "That piece of sheepskin is big. Maybe the hatter could cut out two hats, instead of one."

The customer thought long and hard about the matter and returned to the hatter. "Tell me, hatter," he said. "Could you cut two hats out of that piece of sheepskin?"

"Why not? Of course I could," answered the hatter.

"If you could, then sew two hats," the customer said. Then he left.

The customer walked on for a while, and then he started thinking again. He returned to the hatter and asked, "Hatter, could you perhaps sew three hats from that piece of sheepskin?"

"Why not?" the hatter replied. "I'll sew three."

The customer was overjoyed. Pushing his luck, he asked, "Could you perhaps sew four hats?"

"I'll sew four hats for you," answered the hatter.

"What about five?"

"Yes, I can sew five hats."

"Then sew five hats for me."

The customer left but returned again after getting only halfway home.

"Hatter, could you perhaps sew six hats?"

"I could sew six hats."

"Could you sew seven? Or perhaps you could sew eight hats?"

"Well, why not? I could sew eight hats," said the hatter.

"Then sew eight hats for me."

"Very well, I'll sew eight hats. Come get your order in a week."

After a week had passed, the customer went to the hatter to get his order. "Are my hats ready?" he asked.

"They're ready," the hatter answered. He called to his apprentice and said, "Go bring this customer his hats."

The apprentice came immediately, carrying eight little hats. None of them would fit onto a head, but they might fit onto an apple.

The customer looked at them in amazement. "What's this?" he asked.

"These are the hats you ordered," replied the hatter.

"But why are they so small?"

"Take a moment to think about it, and see if you can come up with the answer," said the hatter.

The customer took the eight little hats and left. Puzzled, the customer started thinking. "Why are these hats so small? Why?"

Do you know the answer?

KNOW-IT-ALL TANGIK*

*T*here once lived a woman named Tangik. Whatever was said to her, she answered, "I know, I know!"

One day before leaving for the field, Tangik's husband said to his wife, "I'd like to have a taste of *dolma*.** I haven't eaten any *dolma* for a long time."

Know-It-All Tangik didn't know how to prepare *dolma*, so she had to go to Tello, her neighbor, to ask for help.

"*Akhchi* (Miss) Tello, how is *dolma* prepared?"

"First you have to cut up the meat," Tello began explaining.

"I know!" Tangik hurried to answer with great dignity.

"Then you must put the meat in a copper saucepan."

"I know."

"Add a little salt and pepper."

"I know, I know."

"Cut up some onion finely. Add some coriander and mint. . . ."

"I know, I know."

"Stuff grape leaves with the mixture and then roll them up. Put the rolls in a copper saucepan."

"I know, I know."

"Well, since you know everything already, do it your way. Why did you come to me pretending not to know anything?" Tello asked angrily.

"Is anything else needed? Is that all?" Tangik asked cautiously. Then Tangik decided that she would prepare such tasty *dolma* that her husband would lick his fingers in satisfaction.

Tello noted that Tangik had too high an opinion of herself, so Tello said, "There is one more thing. Take a piece of dry dung and put it into the saucepan on top of the *dolma*. Let it stew well."

Tangik couldn't contain herself and said, "I know, I know. I already know."

Tangik left to prepare the *dolma*. Tello cried after her. "When the smell of dung fills the air, you'll know that the *dolma* is ready."

---

*Pronounced Taneek.

**Dolma* is an Armenian national dish that consists of grape leaves or vegetables stuffed with ground meat, spices, and rice or bulgur (cracked wheat).

THE TALE ABOUT
A LAZY MAN

*T*here once lived a peasant who had a son. The lad had a reputation for being an idler. It was even rumored that he was too lazy to get up to get himself a glass of water.

One day the boy saw some oxen being driven past their home. "Father, where are they driving the oxen?" asked the lazy son.

"They're driving them to the field to plow, Son," answered his father.

"Father, put me on an ox tomorrow, and take it to the field. But mind that you don't drive the ox too hard."

"All right, Son."

The next morning the peasant took his son to the field. When lunchtime approached, the lazy son said, "I want to eat."

"Since that is the case, Son, get down from the ox. The ox can go to pasture, and I'll go get our lunch."

"No, I won't get down."

The peasant left his son alone. The lazy lad looked around and saw that there wasn't a soul in sight. He decided to drive the oxen around the field. "Let's see whether or not I can get them to move," he thought.

Connected to the plowshare, the oxen moved from the spot where they had been standing and soon halted. The lazy son beat them with a switch, but they didn't budge.

He dismounted. "I'll have a look and find out what the plowshare has caught on and why the oxen have stopped," he said.

He dug a hole in the soil with his hands. In the soil he found forty copper pitchers full of gold. Four gold weights had been placed on top of the gold. The lad dug a hole and buried the four gold weights. Then he sat on top of the treasure.

A little while later, he noticed that the village elder and an errand boy were walking past the field. "If I give the elder the gold, he'll buy oxen and sheep, and then he'll put me to work," thought the lad. "Still, I'd better call the village elder over and give him the gold."

"Hey, elder, come here!" the lazy lad shouted.

"Elder, let's go and find out what that lazybones wants," said the errand boy.

"The heck with him, the idler," answered the elder. "Let's go our own way. Don't pay any attention to him."

The lazy lad wouldn't give up. "Come, come here, elder!"

Finally, the elder gave in and went over to the peasant's son.

Meanwhile, the lazy lad reconsidered his decision to give the elder the gold. "Elder, you are the most important person in the village. Tell me, how is our black ox related to the reddish-brown ox?"

The elder gave the idler a good thrashing for wasting his time and then left.

The lad began thinking again. "I'll taste of grief because of this money. I didn't give the gold to the elder, and he entertained me with his fists. I'd better call him back and give him the gold."

"Elder, come here!" he shouted again.

"Elder, let's go back. Apparently, he didn't call you without reason," said the errand boy.

The elder and the errand boy returned, but the lazy lad began reconsidering his decision again. "Why should I give away the gold? What fool gives away gold?"

"What do you want, fool?" asked the elder.

"Although you are the elder," said the idler, "it never occurred to you to guess that our black ox is related to the uncle of the reddish-brown ox."

The elder became even angrier, and once again he thrashed the lazy lad. After doing so, the elder mounted his horse, and he and the errand boy rode away.

The lazy lad saw his father coming. He wiped away his tears.

The father came up to his son and said, "Come here, Son, let's have a bite to eat."

"I'm not leaving this spot. You come to me."

"That's the plowed field," said the father. "How can we eat there?"

"Do as you wish, but I'm not leaving this spot."

The father went over to his son and saw that the boy was sitting on a clump of grass and that he had dug the earth all around him.

After they had eaten their lunch, the father said, "Get up, Son. Let's go and plow the second half of the field."

"Go by yourself," said the son. "I'm not moving from this spot."

The father plowed the second half of the field. After the plowing was done, he came to his son and said, "It's getting dark. Get up! Let's go home."

"Go home alone, Father. I'm not going."

"If you don't want to go home, you don't have to. But the wolves will come and tear you to pieces."

The lazy son took fright. "Father, listen and I'll tell you something. First, lift me up. Do you see these pitchers? They're full of gold. Keep them for yourself. But I'll take these four gold weights to the king. Go get the cart and take the gold home."

The father got the cart and loaded it with gold. The lazy son took the blanket out of the cart and wrapped the four gold weights in it. Then they set out for home. The lazy lad's mother and father hid the gold.

The wife saw that her husband was unhappy and asked, "Husband, why are you down in the mouth? Today is a day for celebration and joy."

"Oh, there were four gold weights in the ground, too," said the husband, "and our lazy-bones rolled them up in the cart blanket with the intention of taking them to the king. When the king comes here, I'm afraid that he'll take all of our gold away, not just the gold weights."

"Don't grieve. I'll take the gold weights away from our son. Now go to bed."

While the lazy son slept, his mother took a pitcher and broke it. She sprinkled the broken pottery inside the cart blanket and removed the gold weights, which she hid.

In the morning the lazy lad awoke. Unwashed, without shoes, and in his nightclothes, he appeared before the king.

"What do you want, lazybones?" asked the king.

"I brought you a gift." Turning to the nazir, the king's official, the lad said, "Untie the bundle."

The nazir untied the bundle and saw the broken pottery inside. "Why did you bring this, lazybones?"

"So that you would have accurate weights for a pound, a half pound, a half liter, and a liter."

The king got angry and said, "Take him away."

The guards took the lazy lad away and put him in prison.

Then the king said to his servants, "Someone has played a trick on him. Go see what he's doing in prison."

The servants went to the prison and saw that the lazy son was weighing the fragments of pottery in his hands.

The king ordered that the lazy lad be brought before him. The servants did as he ordered.

"Why do you weigh the pieces of pottery?" asked the king.

The lad had been racking his brains in prison to understand why such large weights were suddenly so small.

He decided not to tell the king that he had brought him gold weights. "Oh, king, I was trying to decide how your mother could have given birth to a child with a head as big as yours."

"Take that half-wit away," roared the angry king. "Throw him on some hay and set it afire."

The servants led the lazy lad away. They threw him on top of a pile of hay and set it afire.

Gasping for breath, the lad begged, "Your Majesty, tell them to pull me out of the fire and I'll tell you the truth."

"Pull him out," barked the king.

The servants dragged the lazy lad to the king. "Well, tell the truth."

Meanwhile, the lad had reconsidered his decision to tell the truth. "King, you mustn't suffocate a person with smoke. It's never been done before," said the lazy lad.

The king's advisors said, "It's a sin to punish a half-witted person. Let him go."

The king did as they advised. "Clear out of here," he said to the lazy lad.

The lazy lad thought over what had happened to him. After he arrived home, he said to his father, "It's time for us to manage our own household. Buy a cow, an ox, and a sheep. We'll take care of them."

The father saw that finally his son had seen reason. He arranged for his son to marry a beautiful girl. Everyone had a fine time at the wedding celebration.

They attained their heart's desire. May we attain our heart's desire, too.

Three apples fell from heaven—one for the taleteller and two for the audience.

DON'T OVERSTAY YOUR VISIT

A man came to visit his friend. Happy to see one another, the visitor and his host embraced. They kissed and began asking one another about the state of the other's health, as well as about the health of the other's wife and children. They scarcely knew how to express their joy at seeing one another.

The host threw out the welcome mat and asked how his guest had happened to come and how he had happened to remember them.

"Wife," the host shouted, "get the bed ready for our guest. Order the servants to kill a chicken. Offer our guest some wine. Make some strong tea, and prepare a meal."

The wife made up the guest's bed. On it, she placed a beautiful Karabakh rug that was decorated with roses. On top of the rug she placed the mattress, and on top of the mattress a blanket and a pillow. Then she invited the guest to be seated.

After a day had passed, the hosts removed the pillow. After the passage of two days, they removed the blanket. After the third day, the hosts removed the mattress. On the fourth day the guest began bidding his hosts good-bye and preparing to leave.

Alarmed, the master of the house asked, "Why are you leaving so soon? What happened? How did we displease you? Who offended you? Who said, 'Giddy-up' to your donkey? Don't leave. Stay a bit longer."

"You did nothing wrong," answered the guest. "But I'm not leaving too soon. I should have left the day you took away the pillow."

THE SEARCH FOR A LUMMA (PENNY)

A stingy man heard that there was a man even stingier than he was, so he set out to find out what the other stingy man was like.

Late that night he reached the home of the man reputed to be stingier than he was. He noticed that his stingy rival was turning down the wick of the kerosene lamp and was checking his daily expenses by a scanty light. He was writing and crossing something out. It turned out that he was short a single *lumma*, or penny, and didn't know what he had spent it on.

The stingy man knocked on the door. His rival opened the door and invited the guest into the house. Then he began calculating again.

"Why did you turn down the wick of the lamp?" the stingy guest asked his host.

"If I hadn't turned down the wick, I would have burned too much kerosene."

The guest was amazed at his host's frugality. The guest proceeded to take off his trousers. After taking off his trousers, he sat down on an ottoman.

Dawn came. The host kept checking his expenses. Suddenly, he raised his head and noticed his guest sitting there without his trousers on.

"Why have you taken off your trousers?"

"What kind of question is that? If I keep my pants on, they'll wear out."

The stingy host was struck by his guest's answer. "Yes, indeed, you are stingier than I am," he said. "I economize on kerosene, but you are reluctant to sit down unnecessarily for fear of wearing out your trousers."

YOU REAP WHAT YOU SOW

*I*n the olden days there lived a good-for-nothing woman. One day the woman's mother-in-law became ill and took to her bed. The mother-in-law had a hankering for shashlik, a dish composed of broiled chunks of meat on a skewer.

"Daughter-in-law," she called to her son's young wife, "I'd like to have a bit of shashlik. Please prepare some shashlik for me."

The daughter-in-law didn't answer. Displeased and pouting, she went outside. She caught some frogs in a stream, stuck the frog's meat onto a skewer, and put the skewer into the *tonir*, a clay oven in the ground. After it had cooked, the daughter-in-law put the frog's meat on a piece of bread and gave it to her mother-in-law.

The poor woman took the pieces of meat and ate them. She knew right away that it was frog's meat.

"Listen here, daughter, you gave me frog's meat to eat. I pray to God that in your old age you are treated the same way you treated me," said the mother-in-law. After uttering these words, the old woman died.

Many years passed. The daughter-in-law's eldest son married. The good-for-nothing daughter-in-law had a daughter-in-law of her own. Her son's wife was as gentle as an angel.

Now a mother-in-law herself, the good-for-nothing woman caught a cold and took to her bed. Day and night her daughter-in-law was by her side. The girl looked after her and fulfilled her every desire. She gave her mother-in-law medicine. She prepared a rice broth and fed her mother-in-law with a spoon. In short, she took care of the sick woman just as tradition and humanity dictated.

One day the sick woman had a hankering for shashlik. "Daughter-in-law," she said, "I would like to have some shashlik. Please broil several pieces of meat for me."

The kind daughter-in-law immediately sent her husband to market and ordered him to buy a good cut of mutton. She cut the meat into pieces, chopped up an onion, and put the meat and onion onto a skewer. Then she placed the skewer into a hot *tonir*, or clay oven. She turned the skewer several times so that the shashlik wouldn't burn and removed it from the *tonir* several times to see if it was done.

Finally, she took out the skewer and was stunned and confused. Instead of mutton, frog's meat was strung on the skewer. Unable to understand what had happened, the poor young woman froze with the shashlik in her hand.

She threw out the frog's meat and sent her husband to the market again for mutton. Once again she cut up the meat, put it on a skewer, and placed the skewer in the *tonir*. She took the shashlik out a little later and saw that once again the mutton had turned into frog's meat.

Meanwhile, impatient with her daughter-in-law's tardiness, the good-for-nothing woman shouted, "Why are you dawdling? Bring the shashlik here, and make it snappy!"

"Mother," said the kind daughter-in-law, "do you know what happened? I put the mutton on a skewer, and the mutton turned into frog's meat. I don't understand at all what is going on."

"Bring the frog's meat here, Daughter," sighed the good-for-nothing woman. "Bring it here, and I'll eat it. The frog's meat is payment for my sins."

It is not without reason that people repeat the old proverb: "You reap what you sow."

THE GREEDY PRIEST

*T*here once lived a poor man. One morning he took a pickax and set out to root out tree stumps. He dug up a stump and found gold under it. As he began digging again, he thought, "How can I transport the gold home?"

He stood by the side of the road and saw the priest coming down the road driving seven mules.

"What good luck!" thought the poor man. "He has mules. He'll help me take the gold home safely, and he won't say anything to anyone about it."

As soon as the priest drew near, the poor man said, "What good luck that we met, Father!"

"Why is that?"

"Dear little Father, before his death my grandfather buried all our gold in the forest. Today I dug it up. I've been standing beside the road for seven days. Many people passed by, but I was afraid to trust the first person I met. But I trust you, Father. You are a holy man. You will keep my secret."

"What are you waiting for, son?" shouted the priest.

They agreed that the priest would transport the gold and would take seven gold coins for his services.

They went into the forest and loaded the sacks of gold onto the seven mules. They fit perfectly. Then they set out for home.

On the way, the priest was seized with doubt. "Son, my share is exceedingly small," he commented.

"All right, then, you may have the load on one of the mules for yourself. Drive on."

They traveled a little farther, and doubt seized the priest again. "Son, my share is exceedingly small."

"Father, take the loads on two of the mules for yourself, and drive on quickly."

They went a little farther, and once again the priest began attempting to get a larger portion of the gold. "Son, my share is still exceedingly small."

"Father, take the loads on five of the mules, and drive on!"

A little later the greedy priest started complaining again. "Son, after all, my share is still small."

"Then take all seven loads of gold, Father, but just hurry up."

They came to a spring, where they stopped. The poor man was tormented by thirst. He took out a gold cup that he had found when he was digging up the treasure. He scooped up some water with the cup and drank it.

"Son, give me the cup," said the priest. "I want to drink, too."

After the priest took a drink of water, he tucked the cup into his bosom and said, "I am a priest, so I need the cup more than you do."

Finally, the poor man got angry. He grabbed a fistful of earth and threw it into the priest's face.

The priest was blinded in both eyes and sat down by the side of the road wiping the dirt from his eyes.

The poor man decided not to give the priest anything at all because of his greed. He took the mules and the gold cup and left the priest sitting there. To this day the poor man is wealthy and is living in clover, but the greedy priest is living no better than he was living that fateful day.

LAZY TIUNI AND URI THE SLUG

A husband and wife lived in a small village. The husband's name was Lazy Tiuni, and the wife's name was Uri the Slug. For days on end Tiuni and Uri didn't do anything. They just slept. They were too lazy to boil water for tea and too lazy even to get out of bed to drink the tea.

They had a donkey, but it was Tiuni's parents who fed it. After Tiuni's parents died, the lazy couple continued living as they had, doing nothing.

The inside of the house looked worse with each passing day. Dishes and clothes were unwashed and thrown about. The donkey and garden went untended, and nothing was ever repaired. The yard was a sight to behold. Broken crockery and abandoned tools were scattered everywhere.

The couple's neighbors decided to teach them a lesson. They decided to pretend to bury them alive so that they wouldn't be a bad example to the young people of the community. Pretending to believe that the lazy couple was dead, they placed them on an oxcart and covered them with an old, worn rug. Then they transported them to the cemetery. Too indifferent and lazy to react, Tiuni and Uri lay still in the cart.

On the way to the cemetery, Uri felt sick because of the burning sun. She threw off the rug that covered her. As the oxcart approached the cemetery, Tiuni and Uri started moaning and groaning.

At that moment a horseman appeared at the cemetery gate and asked, "Where are you taking those people?"

"These people are idlers. We're going to bury them so that they won't be a bad influence on our young people," answered one of the peasants.

"Even if we don't bury them, they don't have any bread to eat, and in the end they'll die of hunger," remarked another peasant.

The horseman felt sorry for the lazy couple. "Don't bury them alive," he said. "I'll give them some wheat so that they'll have something to eat."

Having heard the horseman's words, Tiuni cried, "Is the wheat threshed, or must someone thresh it?"

"And will the bread be baked or not?" Uri the Slug asked in turn.

"Is it possible that such lazy people can be found on this earth?" exclaimed the surprised horseman. After asking that question, he galloped away, leaving Tiuni and Uri to their fate.

THE PITCHER OF GOLD

*T*his story was handed down to me from our elders. The elders heard it from their grandfathers, and their grandfathers heard it in turn from their elders.

Once upon a time, there lived a poor farmer, who had only a small plot of land and a pair of oxen.

One winter the poor farmer's oxen died. When spring came and the time came to plow and plant, the farmer couldn't work without his oxen, so he rented his land to a neighbor.

When the neighbor was plowing, his plow suddenly struck something hard. He looked and saw a big clay pitcher full of gold.

He left the oxen and plow and ran to the owner of the land. "Listen, I found a pitcher of gold on your land," he said. "Come, take it away."

"No, brother, that gold isn't mine," said the poor farmer. "You rented the land from me and plowed it, so everything in the land is yours. If you found gold, it is yours. Take it."

The farmer and the man who found the gold began arguing. They kept repeating that the gold belonged to the other. The argument became heated, and a fight broke out. Finally, the two men went to the king with their complaint.

When the king heard about the pitcher of gold, his eyes began burning with greed. "The gold belongs to neither one of you. You found the pitcher of gold in my land, so the gold is mine."

The king hurried with his retinue to the field where the gold had been found. He ordered the pitcher to be opened and saw that it was full of snakes.

Angry and horrified, the king returned to his palace and ordered the impertinent farmers, who had dared to deceive him, to be punished.

"Your Majesty, may you live long," the unfortunate farmers cried. "Why do you want to kill us? There are no snakes in our pitcher. There is gold in the pitcher—only gold!"

The king sent his people to check on the truth of their statement. His people went to the field, looked in the pitcher, and saw only gold. They returned to the king and said, "We found gold in the pitcher."

"Bah, I probably didn't look in the right pitcher or didn't understand what I was seeing," the amazed king thought to himself.

Once again the king went to the field and opened the pitcher. Once again, the pitcher was full of snakes.

"What sort of wonder is this?" asked the king. But no one could understand what was happening.

The king summoned the wise men of his kingdom to gather at the palace. "Explain what sort of wonder this is, wise men," the king ordered. "Some farmers found a pitcher of gold in the earth. When I look into the pitcher, there are snakes in the pitcher. When the farmers look into the pitcher, the pitcher is full of gold. What can it mean?"

"Don't get angry, Your Majesty, when you hear our words. The pitcher of gold was bestowed on the poor farmers as a reward for their hard work and honesty. When they look in the pitcher, they find gold as a reward for honest labor. But when you go there and attempt to steal another man's happiness and good fortune, you find snakes instead of gold."

The king shuddered. He failed to find a single word in reply.

"Very well," he said at last. "Now decide to which one of the farmers the gold belongs."

"It belongs to the owner of the land, of course," exclaimed the farmer who had plowed up the pitcher.

"No, it belongs to the one who plowed the land," objected the owner of the land.

Once again the squabble began anew.

"All right, wait a minute!" The wise men stopped the quarrel. "Do you have any children, perhaps a son or a daughter?"

It turned out that one farmer had a son and the other had a daughter.

The wise men decided that the farmers should arrange a marriage between their children and give them the pitcher of gold as a wedding gift.

The parents of the young people agreed, and everyone was happy. The quarrel ended, and there was a wedding celebration.

They celebrated the marriage for seven days and seven nights. The farmers gave the pitcher of gold, which they had received as a gift for their hard work and honesty, to their children. The gold went to the newlyweds, and the snakes went to the greedy king.

LAZY HOORY

*T*here once lived a woman who had an only daughter. She named the girl Hoory. Hoory was such a lazybones, such a do-nothing and shirker of hard work that whatever occupied her daily hours, she never accomplished anything.

Why should I work?

Why should I strain?

To me work is a pain.

Work just brings care.

Work brings no joy.

I'd rather party

And dance with the boys.

I'd rather sit

And dangle my legs.

I'd rather eat

Than live by my wit.

And whenever sleep beckons,

I'd rather dream

On a moon beam.

The neighbors called the girl Lazy Hoory because of her behavior.

One day Hoory's mother was praising her do-nothing daughter to the world. "Hoory can do everything. She does beautiful needlework. She knits and spins. She cuts out patterns and sews. And she knows how to prepare tasty meals and how to warm the heart with a tender word. Whoever marries her will never regret it."

A young merchant heard the mother's words and thought. "That's the girl for me!"

He went to Hoory and courted her. Soon they were married, and he brought his new bride to his house.

After some time had passed, the merchant brought home a big bale of wool. He asked Hoory to stretch and comb it and spin it into yarn while he was away on business. He told Hoory that he would take the yarn she had spun to other countries and sell it.

"If all goes well and you do a good job, perhaps we'll get rich," he said. And then he left.

After he had gone, Hoory set about her usual business, that is, doing nothing.

One day she went strolling along the riverbank. Suddenly, she heard some frogs croaking, "Croak, croak."

"Hey, frogs," cried Lazy Hoory, "if I bring you a bale of wool, will you comb it and spin it into yarn?"

"Croak, croak," was the reply.

It seemed to Hoory that the frogs' croaking meant "yes." Rejoicing that she had found someone to do her work for her, Hoory ran home.

Soon she returned to the riverbank with the bale of wool her husband had left and threw it into the water.

"Here's your work. Comb the wool and spin it into yarn. I'll come back in a few days to take the yarn and sell it in the marketplace."

Several days passed. Hoory came to the frogs. The frogs croaked as usual, "Croak, croak!"

"Why do you keep croaking 'yes, yes,' frogs? Where's my yarn?"

The frogs just continued croaking in reply. Hoory looked around and noticed green slime and algae on the stones by the riverbank.

"Oh, what have you done? Not only did you comb my wool and spin it into yarn, you wove a carpet for yourselves, too!" Hoory grabbed her head by placing her hands on her rosy cheeks and began crying.

"All right, let it be as it is. You keep the rug for yourselves, but give me the money for the wool."

She wept and demanded money from the frogs. She became so distracted that she waded into the water without noticing what she was doing in her despair.

Suddenly, she stubbed her toe on something hard. She bent over and raised a gold nugget from the bottom of the river.

Hoory was overjoyed. She thanked the frogs and went home with her gold nugget.

When the merchant returned from his business trip, he saw a big gold nugget sitting on a shelf in his house. He was amazed. "Listen, wife, where did the gold nugget come from?" he asked.

Hoory told him that she had sold the wool to the frogs and that she had received gold for the wool.

Hoory's husband was delighted. In celebration he invited his mother-in-law to his house and gave her many gifts. He began praising her and thanking her for raising such a clever daughter and such a gifted worker.

His mother-in-law was a shrewd woman. She immediately grasped that something wasn't right, and it didn't take her long to get to the bottom of the matter. She was afraid that now her son-in-law would give her daughter some new task and that everything that had been so cleverly hidden would be brought to light.

At that moment a beetle flew into the room where the celebration in honor of Hoory was taking place. The beetle flew here and there above peoples' heads and buzzed loudly.

Suddenly, Hoory's mother got up and greeted the beetle. "Hello, hello, dear Auntie. My poor little Auntie, you worked so hard and you were burdened by so many cares! And what was it all for? Why did you do it, why?"

Her words penetrated her son-in-law like a bolt of lightning. "Mama, is everything all right? What are you talking about? How could the beetle be your little Auntie?"

"Listen to me, Son," said the merchant's mother-in-law. "You know I have no secrets from you. You are like my own son, my own flesh and blood. It's hard to imagine, but it's true. This beetle is my aunt. She was forced to work, day in and day out. The more work she had, the more diligently she labored. She became smaller and smaller until finally she turned into a beetle. In our family it could happen to any one of us, because we are very hardworking. Those of us who work too much shrink and turn into beetles."

After her son-in-law heard these words, he forbade his wife to do any work at all for fear that she would turn into a beetle, as her aunt had.

Four Amusing Tales

THE GREATEST SORROW IN THE WORLD

A thief who had been caught stealing was led to the sultan. The sultan ordered that the criminal be tied to the pillar of shame on the town square so that every passer-by could spit at him.

Several days later the sultan went to the town square. He approached the pillar of shame and asked the thief, "Well, is there any sorrow in the world greater than the one that has befallen you?"

"There is, oh Sovereign," answered the thief.

"What on earth could be worse than being tied to this pillar?" asked the sultan.

"The greatest sorrow in the world, Sovereign, is when a guest comes to visit and you have nothing to feed him," replied the thief.

THE DEAF MAN, THE CRIPPLE, AND THE BALD MAN

A deaf man, a cripple, and a bald man were walking down the road together. Suddenly, the deaf man said, "I hear a wolf howling!"

"Let's run!" the cripple man exclaimed.

"You are speaking such nonsense that you're making my hair stand on end," the bald man replied.

Grandfather of Hopartsi, village in Lori Region, holding his grandsons.

Girl dressed in festive costume for the Vardavar festival celebrating the Transfiguration of Christ at Haghardzin Monastery.

Children in Yerevan sitting on a wall and eating ice cream.

Woman spinning.

Woman of Ashnak, a village in Aragatsotn Region near Mount Aragats.

Women of Bjni making *lavash* (flat bread) in a *tonir* (clay underground oven).

Horseman from Hadrut Region in southern Karabakh.

Beekeeper from Hadrut Region in the mountainous southernmost area of Karabakh.

Sculptor Varbed Vahan in his Yerevan studio.

Richly ornamented *khachkars* (crosses) at Saghmosavank Monastery in Aragatsotn Region.

A water fountain at Moush in western Armenia.

Sanahin Bridge in Lori Region, an important secular monument of the twelfth century.

Boys of Ashnak, a village in Aragatsotn Region near Mount Aragats.

Villagers of Goshavank in Tavoush Region.

Hayrik Mouradian Children's Traditional Song and Dance Ensemble.

The Church of St. Hripsimé, built in Echmiadzin in AD 618 to commemorate the martyrdom of the beautiful nun Hripsimé, who was tortured to death for resisting the advances of Diocletian and Tiridates III.

Dadivank Monastery in the Nagorno-Karabakh Republic (Artsakh), the largest monastic complex in Nagorno-Karabakh. The main church was constructed in 1214 by Queen Arzou-Khatoun, and the monastery is working today. It is built over the grave of a man named Dadi (pronounced "dodi"), who preached Christianity in the area in the first century.

Haghardzin Monastery in the Tavoush Region, a thirteenth-century complex located in a rain forest.

Amberd Fortress (eleventh to thirteenth centuries), in the Aragatsotn Region, a fortress complex with a church, located on the slopes of Mount Aragats.

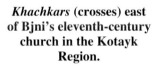

Khachkars (crosses) east of Bjni's eleventh-century church in the Kotayk Region.

Old Urartian Van Fortress in western Armenia (now Turkey) near Lake Van, where in 1915 the Armenians defended themselves against the Turks.

View from ninth-century Kachaghakaberd (Fortress of the Magpies) in Askeran Region of Karabakh. The fortress is poetically situated on a white rock in the forest.

Tutoo Choor wedding celebration in Aragatsotn Region on the southern slopes of Mount Aragats.

View of Mount Ararat (Masis) from Mt. Aragats.

GOD, YOU DIDN'T UNDERSTAND ME

A tired peasant was climbing a mountain with a heavy load on his back.

"Lord," he prayed, "either relieve me of my load or take my soul and free me from this torment."

At that moment the peasant came upon a merchant whose donkey had died while on the journey. The merchant took off the donkey's *palan*, a felt saddle used on pack animals. He placed the *palan* on the peasant, and he forced the peasant to carry the donkey's load in addition to his own.

"God, apparently I failed to convince you of my bitter fate. Or perhaps you just didn't understand me," said the peasant.

THE PEASANT AND HIS ROOF

A poor peasant lived with his family in a dilapidated house with a flat earthen roof. In time cracks began appearing in the roof. Every time that he saw a crack, the peasant repaired it with some clay.

One day he returned home from the field and saw that the roof had collapsed and that his children were injured and bruised.

"Oh, you ill-fated roof. Couldn't you have warned me that you were going to tumble down?" asked the peasant.

"How many times did I open my mouth to tell you about it?" asked the roof. "Every time I opened my mouth, you daubed clay onto it. You didn't want to listen to me, so who, then, is to blame?"

PART 5

WITS AND DIMWITS

THE GOLDEN APPLE

*T*here once lived a king who one day out of boredom took it into his head to amuse himself by staging a contest. He sent trumpeters throughout his kingdom to make an announcement to the public.

"Countrymen, whoever tells a lie so great that the king believes it to be a lie will be given a golden apple."

Princes, merchants, and all sorts of people came to the king from all corners of his kingdom. None of them could satisfy the king.

Finally, a poor man carrying a big pitcher in his hand came to the king.

"What do you want?" asked the king.

"May you have a long life, Your Majesty," answered the poor man. "I have come for my money. You owe me a pitcher full of gold."

"You're lying! I don't owe you anything," answered the king.

"Did you say I'm lying? Then give me the golden apple if I'm lying."

The king understood the poor man's cunning and began changing his story. "No, you're not lying. You're right," he said to the poor man.

"If I'm not lying, then pay your debt."

If he said that the man was lying, the king would have to give him the golden apple. If he said that the man wasn't lying, the king would have to give the man a pitcher of gold. The king weighed the worth of the apple and the worth of the pitcher of gold, and decided he would lose less by declaring that the man was lying. That is how it came about that the king had to give the poor man the golden apple.

THE MASTER AND THE HIRED MAN

*T*here once lived two brothers, and they were very poor. When their poverty become dire, they decided that the younger brother would stay at home while the older brother got a job and sent his salary home. They did as planned. The younger brother stayed at home and managed the house and the little farm, and the older brother went to a foreign land, where he applied for a job working for a wealthy master.

According to their agreement, the time of the older brother's job would expire in spring when the cuckoo began singing. The master set the following condition. "If one of us gets angry before the time agreed upon is up, he will pay a forfeit. If you get angry, you will pay me a thousand *dram*s.* On the other hand, if I get angry, I'll pay you the same amount."

"But I don't have a thousand *dram*s," said the older brother.

"Don't worry. Instead of giving me a thousand *dram*s, you will work for me for nothing for ten years."

At first the young man was afraid of entering into such an agreement, but in the end he thought it over and gave in. "Whatever he says, I won't get angry. And if the master loses his temper, he'll have to pay me as we agreed," the older brother thought to himself. Thus, he began working for the master.

The next day the master sent his worker to the field early in the morning. "Go to the field and begin mowing as soon as it gets light. Come back when it gets dark."

The young man worked all day in the field. When he returned home tired, the master asked, "Why have you come home?"

"What do you mean? The sun set, so I came back," answered the young man.

"You can't do that! I told you to mow while it was light. It's true that the sun has set. But its sister, the moon, came up. The moon doesn't shine so badly either."

"How is it possible?" asked the amazed worker. "How could you possibly ask me to work day and night?"

"Apparently, you are angry with me," said the master.

"I'm not angry. It's just that I'm tired. I need to rest a little," answered the young man, his speech faltering for fear that he would have to pay a thousand *dram*s. Tired and unsteady on his feet, he went back to the field to work.

He mowed until the moon went down, but right after that the sun came up. Exhausted, the young man fell to the ground. He began to revile the master. "May your field and your bread be cursed, as well as your money."

The master appeared from nowhere after the young man had uttered these words. "What's the matter? Are you angry? Keep in mind that our agreement can't be broken. Don't wag your tongue about my acting illegally or treating you badly unless you mean it."

The young man felt like he was caught between two fires. He didn't have a thousand *dram*s to give to the master, and to work for such a man for ten years was unthinkable.

The young man thought and thought about what he could do. Finally, he gave the master a promissory note for the thousand *dram*s, and he returned to his home empty-handed.

"Well, how did it go?" his younger brother asked.

The older brother told him everything that had happened.

"That's not so bad. Don't be upset," said the younger brother. "You stay home, and I'll go find a job."

The younger brother went to the same wealthy master and asked for work. Once again the master set the condition that the young man work until spring when the cuckoo began singing. If the younger brother got angry, he would have to pay the master a thousand *dram*s or work for him for ten years. If, on the other hand, the master got angry, he would have to pay the worker a thousand *dram*s and release him from work.

"That's too little. If you get angry, you must pay me two thousand *dram*s. And if I get angry, I'll give you two thousand *dram*s or I'll work for you for nothing for twenty years."

"Agreed!" the master exclaimed happily. They struck a bargain, and the younger brother was hired.

The next day when the sun rose, the younger brother was still sleeping.

The master shook him to awaken him. "Excuse me, but soon it will be noon, and you are still lying abed."

"What's the matter? Are you angry?" asked the worker, raising his head.

"I'm not angry," answered the master. "I just wanted to say that you must go to the field to mow hay."

Eventually, the young man got up. He stretched and slowly began putting sandals on his feet.

"Hurry, boy! You mustn't be so slow!"

"What's that? Are you angry?"

"No, and I'm not even thinking of being angry. I just wanted to say that we're late for work."

"That's another matter. Watch out. Keep in mind that our agreement can't be broken."

By the time the younger brother put on his sandals and went to the field, it was afternoon.

"Is it worth working now?" he asked the master. "As you can see, everyone is having lunch. Let's have lunch, too."

They sat down to eat lunch. After lunch, the hired hand said to the master, "We are working people, so we have to take a little nap to acquire the strength to continue." Burying his head in the grass, he fell asleep until evening.

"Listen, boy, aren't you a God-fearing man? It's already getting dark. Everyone else has mown their fields. Only ours remains unmown. May the neck of the person who sent you to me be broken! What sort of punishment is this?" the master said in despair.

"Are you angry?" asked the younger brother, raising his head.

"No, I'm not angry. I just wanted to say that it's getting dark, and it's time to go home."

"That's a different matter. Let's go! But our agreement remains the same."

When they arrived home, a guest was waiting for the master. He sent his hired hand to the farmyard to slaughter one of the sheep for dinner.

"Which one should I slaughter?" asked the younger brother.

"Whichever one you come upon," replied the master.

The hired hand went out into the yard. After some time had passed, people came running to the master to tell him that his hired man had gone crazy and was slaughtering one sheep after another. The master ran out of the house only to see that his entire flock of sheep had been slaughtered.

At that point, the master lost control and began shouting, "May your roof collapse for what you have done!"

"But you said that I should slaughter whichever sheep I came upon. That's just what I did. I haven't done anything wrong," the hired hand answered calmly. Then he added, "I see that you are angry with me."

"No, I'm not angry. But it grieves me that you have destroyed my entire flock for nothing."

"All right. If you're not angry, I'll continue to work."

The younger brother worked in that manner for several months until he had brought the master to the brink of despair. The master decided that he must rid himself somehow of his worker. According to the agreement, the hired man's term was up when the cuckoo began to sing in spring. Meanwhile, winter had just begun and the spring song of the cuckoo was far off.

The master thought and thought about what he could do. He decided to deceive his cunning worker. He took his wife to the forest and lifted her into a tree. He ordered her to sing like a cuckoo as soon as he came to the forest with the hired hand.

Meanwhile, the master hurried home. He ordered his hired hand to get ready to go hunting in the forest with him.

When they entered the forest, the master's wife began to sing, "Cuckoo, cuckoo!"

"Aha! I congratulate you. The cuckoo is singing. Your term of service is up," said the master.

The young man understood right away what his master was doing. "No," he said, "it can't be. Have you ever heard of a cuckoo singing in the middle of winter? I must kill that cuckoo so that we can see what sort of bird it is."

After uttering those words, the young man took aim, directing his rifle to the tree in which the master's wife was sitting.

With a roar, the master rushed at the hired hand. It was only with great difficulty that he persuaded him not to fire.

"May you croak, you swine! You've exasperated me."

"Do I sense that you are angry?" the hired hand asked the master.

"Yes, yes, boy, I'm angry!" came the long-awaited reply. "Come, I'll pay you, and for your part you must leave me in peace. Now I understand the meaning of the old proverb: 'Don't dig a hole for someone else. You may fall into it yourself.'"

---

*The *dram* is the basic Armenian monetary unit.

THE SHOEMAKER'S DEBT

*T*here once lived a shoemaker who owed someone money.

The creditor kept going to the debtor saying, "Listen here, why don't you pay back your debt? Aren't you ashamed? After all, a great deal of time has passed. Don't you have a conscience? Why are you acting so badly? When are you going to give me back my money?"

"Why are you in such a hurry? I'll give the money back," answered the shoemaker.

One day the creditor came to the shop and noticed that the shoemaker wasn't there. Only his apprentices were at work.

"Apprentices, do you know when your master will have some money so that he can pay me back?" asked the creditor.

One of the apprentices gave the following reply. "Take this wooden shoe last.* Throw it into the water. When the last swells up and blossoms into a tree, you will receive your money."

When the shoemaker returned, he asked his apprentices if anyone had come in his absence. The apprentice told him what had happened and what he had said.

The shoemaker got angry and shouted to the apprentice, "Oh, you good-for-nothing! And what if the shoe last blooms when it is placed in water? What then?"

_____

*A last is a wooden block shaped like a foot, on which the shoemaker repairs shoes.

WHEN MY HEART TELLS ME

A certain man borrowed some money from a relative and agreed to return the debt when his heart told him to do so.

Every time his relative asked him to return the money, the debtor answered, "My heart hasn't told me to pay back the debt yet."

Finally, the man's relative was forced to take the matter to court. The debtor announced in court that the agreement between him and his relative was that he should return the money when his heart told him to do so.

"Very well," said the judge. "I order that you be sent to prison immediately. When your heart tells you to return the debt, you'll be released from prison."

THE DONKEY THAT SWALLOWED THE MOON

One night a peasant led his donkey to a pond to take a drink of water. When the donkey's snout came near the water, the reflection of a slipper moon appeared. As the donkey drank, the moon hid behind the clouds.

"Woe is me," exclaimed the peasant. "My donkey has swallowed the moon."

The peasant got a knife and cut open the donkey's belly to release the moon. At that moment, the moon appeared again from behind the clouds.

"There is the moon—back in the sky. That means that my donkey really did swallow the moon," declared the silly peasant.

THE NE'ER-DO-WELL SON

*L*ong ago there lived a king who had three sons. When the sons were small, they lived in peace and harmony. But after they grew up, there was discord among them. Each day there was a racket, a fight, a squabble—in short, they couldn't get along with one another.

One day they went to their father and said, "Father, since we don't get along with one another, we should part company. What do you think?"

"That's your business, my sons," said their father. "If you don't get along, live apart. I'll give each of you a share of your inheritance. Take it and build your nests. Live as you wish."

The king gave each of his sons a share of his inheritance and let the boys go. The brothers set up their own households, married, and lived independently of each other.

The eldest of the sons turned out to be a good-for-nothing. Soon he had squandered everything that he had. He went to his father again and kicked up a racket, saying that he had received less than his brothers.

The king had to give him another portion of his inheritance, the same amount of money that he had given his son previously.

The king's son squandered this money, too, and had nothing once again. He went to his father and demanded more money, and again his father gave him what he wanted. Then he squandered the third share of his inheritance, too. He received a fourth portion of money, but he threw it to the winds, just as he had done before. In the end, he was left as naked as a jaybird.

The king's son grew thoughtful. "I think I'll go to God with my complaint. I'll ask him why he keeps punishing me by taking away all my property. He's left me in poverty while my brothers increase their wealth."

The king's son took supplies for several months and equipped himself for a long journey. Then he set out. He walked on for one, two, three, four days. In short, he walked until he came to a forest. In the forest he met a bear that was mangy and wounded.

When the bear caught sight of the king's son, it asked, "Where are you going, Son of the King?"

"I'm going to God with a complaint. I was once wealthy, but everything is gone. I have become a pauper without a crust of bread. Now I'm going to God to ask what sins I'm being punished for."

"If that's the case, I'll tell you about my grief," said the bear. "When you arrive at God's, tell Him about my complaint, too. I've been tormented with sores for many years. Whatever I do, I can't seem to escape this affliction. Please ask God what I can do."

"Don't worry. On my return trip, I'll bring you God's answer."

The king's son walked on until he came to a large town. As he was walking around town, he met a man.

"Hello, Son of the King," said the man.

"Hello," answered the king's son.

"Where are you going?"

"I'm going to God with my complaint."

"If that is the case, tell God about my complaint, too. I have an enormous orchard with unfruitful trees. In spring the trees blossom, but the fruit doesn't last. It withers and dies. Please ask God what I should do."

"Very well," said the king's son, "I'll tell God about your complaint."

After uttering those words, the king's son went on. He kept walking for one, two, and three days until he came to another kingdom.

When the king of that country heard about the king's son, he summoned him. "Who are you?" the king asked. "Where are you headed?"

"I am the son of a king," said the king's son. "I am going to God to lodge a complaint."

"If that is the case, be so kind as to inform God of my complaint, too," said the king. "I have been ruling for many years. However, no matter what I do, no matter what punishment I dream up, I can't rid my country of thieves. Bring my complaint to God, and ask Him what I should do."

"Don't worry, Your Majesty, I'll tell God about your complaint," answered the king's son.

Having uttered those words, he traveled on. He walked one, two, three days, and one, two three weeks. In short, he walked on for a whole month. He walked at night, during the day, in the sunshine, and in the dark.

Finally, he came to the edge of the world. He almost fell into the sea, but luckily God sent an angel to meet him. The angel stood before the king's son and blocked his path.

"Who are you, and where are you going?" asked the angel.

"I am the son of a king," said the ne'er-do-well. "I am going to God with a complaint. I separated from my brothers. They became wealthy on their share of our inheritance, but I squandered everything I had. So I decided to go to God to ask why I have fallen into such misfortune and for what sins I am being punished."

"Would you like to hear my advice?" asked the angel.

"Of course I would," answered the king's son. "That is why I have come here."

"I am God's angel. God sent me to tell you to turn back and you will find your lost wealth."

"Thank God," said the king's son. "I'll do as He has ordered. I have another complaint. On my journey, I met a bear in the forest. The bear was mangy and covered with sores. He asked me where I was going, and I told him that I was going to God with a complaint. The bear asked me to tell God that he had been suffering for many years with sores, regardless of what he did to get rid of them. The bear wanted me to ask God what he should do about his sores."

"The bear must eat a human being. If he does so, his sores will be healed," answered the angel.

"That's not all," said the king's son. "As I was going through a certain town, I met a man who asked me where I was going. I told him that I was going to God with a complaint. He asked me to tell God that he has an orchard, where every type of tree grows. In spring, the trees are covered with blossoms, but the fruit withers and dies soon after it starts growing. The man wanted me to ask God what would help him in his misfortune."

"The man's trees never bear fruit because gold is buried under every tree. If he digs up the gold, his trees will yield fruit."

"That's not all," said the king's son. "When I was passing through a foreign kingdom, the king summoned me and asked where I was going. I told him that I was the son of a king and that I was going to God with a complaint. He asked me to take his complaint to God, too. He said that no matter how many years he ruled and no matter what he did, no matter what punishments he dreamed up, nevertheless he couldn't put an end to theft in his kingdom. He told me to ask God what could be done."

"The king of that country is not a man, but rather the king is a woman," said the angel. "That is why there is no order. The thieves have no fear of her. If a man were king, his word would be law and the theft would end." After uttering those words, the angel disappeared.

Satisfied, the king's son headed home. He walked on and on until he came to the kingdom where the king was a woman dressed in man's clothing. He went to the palace and told about his encounter with the angel.

"You're right," said the king of that country. "I am a woman, and that must be why my word isn't law. If that is the case, marry me and ascend the throne. God must have sent you to me to my great good fortune."

"No, I can't marry you," said the king's son. "I must return to my own country to get back my lost wealth."

After refusing to marry, he went on. He walked until he came to the town where he met the owner of the large orchard. He told the owner everything that he had heard from the angel, and he helped the orchard owner dig up the gold from under the tree roots.

The orchard owner was so happy that he could scarcely feel his legs beneath him. "King's Son," he said, "I would like to tell you something, but I don't know whether or not you'll listen to me."

"Speak," said the king's son. "Why wouldn't I listen to you?"

"You did me a great service by bringing my complaint to God. You've made me rich. I want to repay you for your good deed. I have an only daughter. Marry her and become my son-in-law. I am old, and I don't have long to live. After my death, all of my wealth will become yours, and you'll live splendidly."

"Oh, no," said the king's son. "I can't remain here. I must go to my own country to get back my lost wealth."

The ne'er-do-well son of the king let his good fortune slip through his fingers. He didn't pay any attention to the words of the orchard owner and went his own way. He traveled on until he met the sick bear.

"Well, King's Son, did you bring my complaint to God?" asked the bear.

"Yes, I did," said the king's son, "and God told me what you must do."

"What did God say?"

"He said that you must catch a human being and eat him up. Then you'll be cured."

"If that is the case, I'll eat you up," said the bear. "God sent you to me for that purpose."

The bear attacked the ne'er-do-well son of the king, tore him to pieces, and ate him up. After doing so, the bear was miraculously cured of his illness. Evidently, it was God's will that the ne'er-do-well son of the king end up in the stomach of a mangy bear.

DEATH OR FREEDOM

*T*here once lived a beautiful maiden and a very clever servant. The maiden and the servant fell in love. The maiden's father was a ruler, and he didn't like the servant.

"How on earth can the daughter of a ruler marry a pauper? She'll disgrace me and ruin my honor and dignity. That cannot be. The entire world will put me to shame."

The ruler couldn't calm down. At night he didn't sleep. His wise councilors tried to convince him that it would be wrong to darken and destroy love, that it would be a sin.

Nevertheless, the ruler insisted on his own point of view. "No, and no again! I won't let my daughter marry a servant."

The matter finally reached the courts. The judge decided that the servant shouldn't be punished. The judge ordered that instead lots be drawn and that with the drawing of lots the matter should end. Several people were chosen to prepare two pieces of paper. They were supposed to write "death" on one piece of paper and "freedom" on the other. However, the prince bribed them so that they wrote "death" on both pieces of paper. Whichever piece of paper the servant chose, he would have to die.

The servant drew a lot and quickly swallowed it.

A quarrel ensued. The ruler maintained that "death" had been written on the piece of paper that the servant had swallowed.

"No, the word 'freedom' was written on the paper that I swallowed," said the servant. "To prove it, let's open the box and see what is written on the piece of paper that remains."

The box was opened, and everyone saw that the piece of paper that remained had "death" written on it.

The ruler could no longer offer any objections to his daughter's marriage. The servant married the ruler's daughter, and they are living in happiness and good fortune to this very day.

A TALL, TALL TALE

*O*nce upon a time there lived a man and his wife. They were as poor as poor can be. Their prized possession was a strange, little hen. She bit whoever passed in front of her, and she scratched whoever passed behind her. She was such a savage, nasty-tempered hen that she terrorized the village, and no one dared walk down her street.

Unable to stand it any longer, the villagers went with their complaint to the village elder. The elder summoned the hen's owner and ordered him either to eat the hen for Sunday dinner or to lock her up in the barn so that she would not frighten passers-by.

The owner took pity on the hen. He did not want to eat her. Instead, he locked her up in the barn and caulked up all the chinks so that she couldn't escape.

One day, two days, three days passed. One week, two weeks, in short, an entire month passed. The hen was given neither feed nor water. Her master had forgotten about her.

Then one day the owner suddenly remembered the hen. "Listen, wife," he said. "We must take a look to see how the hen is doing."

"You're right," said his wife. "Go have a look at the hen."

The man opened the barn door, and what did he see?—the barn was full of eggs! An entire mountain of eggs rose up to the roof. The man was so happy that he couldn't feel his legs beneath him.

He ran to tell his wife. The man and woman took a big basket and carried the eggs to the threshing floor of the barn. They harnessed oxen to the threshing board and smashed the eggs to bits. They continued to work until all the eggs were crushed.

Then they glanced around. They saw that little roosters had hatched on one side of the threshing floor and that little hens had hatched on the other side.

On top of the heap of broken eggs, a goose had hatched. The goose took to her heels the moment she saw them. The owner forgot about his chickens and began dashing after the goose. On and on he ran.

Finally, he spied his goose. A stranger had harnessed the bird to a plow and was urging it on. "Hey, brother," he cried. "That's my goose. Why have you harnessed her?"

"Are you sure it's your goose?" asked the man. "I assumed that she didn't belong to anyone, so I harnessed her. Well, if she's yours, take her. And here are two bushels of wheat for the goose as payment for her work."

The owner took the goose and the two bushels of wheat. He poured the wheat into two baskets, covered them tightly, loaded them onto the goose, and drove the goose home.

After returning home, he took the baskets off the goose, and what do you think he saw? On the goose's back, a large wound had opened. The couple couldn't figure out how it had happened. They rushed here, there, and everywhere, first to one neighbor, then to another. No one knew how to help.

Finally, a man advised them to grease the wound with a crushed nut poultice. "You have only to dab on crushed nuts," he said, "and the wound will heal right away."

Unfortunately, nuts were not grown in their country, but nevertheless the couple searched and searched until they came upon an old woman sitting on her porch. "Listen, old woman," the man and his wife said, "for the sake of your soul's salvation, tell us whether or not you have a few nuts. Our goose's back has a terrible wound, and we need some crushed nuts to treat it. For the love of your own dear sons, give us at least one nut."

"My children," said the old woman. "I was still a child when my father brought some nuts back from India. Give me a toothpick. I'll pick my teeth. Maybe a piece of nut got stuck somewhere."

The husband and wife wasted no time. They saw a log lying on the ground, picked it up, and gave it to the old woman.

The old woman stuck the entire log into her mouth, pulled a piece of nut out of a cavity, and gave it to the couple.

The husband and wife were overjoyed. They kissed the old woman's hand, took the little piece of nut, and returned home, where they treated the wound with a paste made from the nut. The wound healed in no time at all.

One day, two days, three days passed. One week, two weeks, three weeks, in short, an entire month passed. On the goose's back a big nut tree began growing, and on the tree were countless nuts.

Everyday the goose went to graze in the field. She returned home in the evening. While she was in the field, shepherds and small children knocked nuts down from the tree. In an attempt to get the nuts, some people threw stones at the tree; some threw twigs; and others threw sod. The twigs and sod stuck to the nut tree, and lo and behold, eventually a green lawn sprawled across the tree on the goose's back.

People began planting gardens and orchards on the lawn. They plowed the earth and sowed barley and wheat. Shepherds led flocks of sheep and herds of cows to pasture there.

One day a man climbed up to the garden on the goose's back. There he picked himself a watermelon. He tried to cut it open to no avail. He stuck his knife deep into the watermelon. "Oh, help, now my knife is stuck!" he cried.

His knife had disappeared completely into the watermelon. There was no possibility of getting it out, so the man climbed into the watermelon in search of his knife. He walked about in the watermelon, but found no knife.

While he was inside the melon, he came upon a shepherd with a staff on his shoulder. "Hey, brother," the shepherd called to him. "Who are you? What on earth are you doing in this watermelon?"

My knife disappeared in here," the man answered. "I'm looking for it. Perhaps I'll find it."

"Foolish man," the shepherd said to him. "Two years ago, my flock of sheep vanished into this watermelon. I have walked my legs off, but I can't find them. And you think you can find a teensy, weensy knife?"

The shepherd's words made the man angry. He rushed at the shepherd, and a fight broke out. The two men began hitting one another. During the fight, the melon rolled and rolled until it fell with a crash from the goose's back onto the ground, where it broke into pieces.

A rabbit jumped out of the watermelon and ran away. A little piece of paper fell from under the rabbit's tail.

Some shepherds standing in the field grabbed the piece of paper. They could not make out what was written on the paper since they didn't know how to read.

After staring at the paper for some time, the shepherds brought it to the village priest, who did know how to read. The priest unrolled the paper and read what was written on it: "This has been a tale, a tall, tall tale."

BROTHER AX

*O*nce upon a time a young man set out for distant lands in search of work. The road led him to a village where his eyes fell on a remarkable scene. People were felling trees with their naked hands.

"Brothers," said the young man, "why are you felling trees with your hands? Don't you have an ax?"

"An ax? What is an ax?" asked the villagers.

The young man pulled an ax out of his belt, and in no time at all he chopped the trees into firewood, which he arranged carefully in a pile.

Witnessing the feat, the residents of the village rushed to their homes shouting, "Hey, come here everyone! Come here and see what Ax-*Dzhan** has done!"

The villagers surrounded the young man who owned the ax. They begged and threatened and promised the young man anything he wanted in exchange for the ax. Finally, they took the ax away from the young man by force and decided to manage the ax themselves.

The village elder was the first one to grab the ax. He swung the ax once and cut off his toes on one foot. Then the elder rushed around the village, crying in pain, "Help! Everyone come here. Ax-*Dzhan* is angry. He has chopped off half my leg!"

The villagers came running and began beating the ax with sticks. They beat it and beat it, but what did the ax care? It lay on the ground just as it had been lying before.

The villagers understood that they were getting nowhere in their punishment of the ax, so they decided to burn it. They piled wood on top of it and set the wood afire. When the fire died down, the villagers rushed to see what had happened to the ax. After scattering the ashes, they found the red-hot metal ax.

"Aha!" they exclaimed. "You've destroyed yourself, Ax-*Dzhan*. See how red you are. We dare say you are ashamed of yourself. It serves you right! You caused much unhappiness and are capable of causing even more. We're going to put you in jail!"

They did as they had decided. They threw the red-hot ax into the village elder's barn. The barn was full of hay. The ax fell onto the hay, and the hay burst into flame. Enormous flames leapt into the heavens.

The villagers took fright and began chasing the young man who had brought the ax to the village. As they were chasing him, they begged, "Young man, come to our aid. We can't manage the ax ourselves. For goodness sake, make your Ax-*Dzhan* listen to reason."

**Dzhan is a title of respect meaning "dear life" or "dear soul." It is pronounced Jhan with "j" as in "jar."

CARNIVAL

*T*here once lived a man and wife who didn't get along very well. Either the husband was calling his wife a fool, or the wife was calling her husband a fool. They lived in never-ending quarrels and brawls.

One day the husband bought a hundred pounds of butter and rice and brought them home.

The wife flew into a rage. "Didn't I tell you that you were a fool? What a simpleton! Why have you bought so much butter and rice? Did you buy enough food to prepare a feast to marry off our son or have a funeral for your father?"

"What are you talking about? What wedding? What funeral? Hide the butter and rice. Put it away until Carnival comes."

The wife calmed down. She took the food and put it away in the house.

Time passed. The wife waited and waited for Carnival to come, but Carnival didn't make an appearance. One day the woman was sitting on a bench in front of the house when she saw a stranger walking down the street.

She waved to the stranger and said, "Hey, brother, come here for a moment."

The lad stopped.

"Listen, brother, is your name Carnival by any chance?"

The lad guessed immediately that the woman's mind was not quite right. "I'll just tell her my name is Carnival, and we'll see what happens," he thought.

"Of course, sister. My name is Carnival."

"You know, Carnival, I just want to tell you that we're not being paid to keep your rice and butter. Aren't you ashamed to take advantage of our kindness? Why has it taken you so long to show up to take your food?"

"Don't get angry, sister. That's why I'm here now. I wasted a lot of time looking for your house, but I finally found it."

"Well, all right, come in and get your food."

The lad went into the house and took the butter and rice. He flung the sacks on his shoulders and left the village.

When her husband returned toward evening, the woman said, "At last your Carnival appeared. I gave him the food and sent him packing."

"What Carnival? What are you talking about, woman? What food?"

"The butter and rice. I looked and saw Carnival walking down the street looking for our house. I called to him. I gave him a good scolding. Let him carry his food on his back all the way home!"

"You astound me with your stupidity, woman. What a simpleton! Didn't I tell you that you were a fool? What road did he take?"

The woman pointed out the road. Her husband saddled the horse and rushed off in pursuit of Carnival.

Meanwhile, having safely slipped away from the village, Carnival stopped to glance around. He saw a horseman riding after him. Carnival immediately grasped that the rider must be the husband of the woman from whom he got the rice and butter, so he hid the sacks in the bushes by the side of the road.

The horseman caught up with Carnival and asked, "Hello, there, friend. Have you by any chance seen a traveler walking down this road?"

"I remember seeing a man."

"Was he carrying something on his back?"

"Butter and rice."

"Aha, that's the one I'm looking for. Did you see him long ago?"

"Yes, rather a long time ago."

"What do you think, brother, will I catch up to him if I gallop a bit faster?"

"Hardly," replied Carnival. "Figure it out for yourself. You are on horseback, and he is on foot. While your horse is moving all of his feet—count them, one-two-three-four, the person you are chasing is running on two feet. To move his feet, he has only to go one-two, one-two. That is faster than you can go by horse, one-two-three-four."

"What should I do?"

"If you want, I'll help you. Leave your horse with me and chase him on foot—one-two, one-two. If you run quickly, you'll undoubtedly catch up with him."

"Yes, yes, indeed. Those are golden words," agreed the foolish husband.

He jumped down from the horse and left the horse with Carnival. Meanwhile, he began pursuing Carnival on foot. As he ran, he kept repeating, "One-two, one-two, one-two."

As soon as the husband had disappeared from view, Carnival got the sacks of butter and rice out from behind the bushes and loaded them onto the horse. He galloped off in the opposite direction.

The foolish husband wandered far and wide, but he met no one. Finally, he returned to the spot where he had left the stranger and his horse. Naturally, there was no trace of man or beast.

When he returned home, there was another brawl. The husband scolded his wife for losing the rice and butter, and the wife scolded her husband for losing the horse.

To this day the husband and wife are squabbling. First, the husband calls his wife a fool, and then she calls him a fool. However, Carnival knows that both of them are fools, and he is chuckling at their expense.

TWO BROTHERS

There once lived two brothers. One was clever, and the other was a fool. The clever brother arranged matters so that the foolish brother had to work not only for himself but for his brother, too.

Finally, becoming exhausted, the foolish brother said in despair, "I don't want to stay with you any longer. Give me my share of our inheritance, and I'll live by myself."

"Very well," said the clever brother. "Today you will drive our herd of cows to the pond. I'll feed them after you drive them home. The part of the herd that goes into the pen will be mine, and the part of the herd that remains outside will be yours."

It was winter, but the foolish brother agreed to the arrangement. He drove the herd to the pond. By the time he returned home, it was quite cold. Sensing the nearness of warmth and the scent of food, the cows quickly entered the pen. Only one ill bull barely dragging its legs was left outside the pen stamping its hooves and lazily scratching. This bull was the foolish brother's inheritance.

The next morning, after tying a rope around the bull's neck, the foolish brother led the bull to market to sell him. The foolish brother had a great deal of difficulty getting the lazy bull to move. "Hey, bull, move those legs. Get going!"

Their road ran by some old ruins. The walls of the ruins echoed the foolish brother's words. "Hey!" shouted the fool.

And he thought that the ruins had returned his greeting. "Hey!"

The foolish brother shouted, "Are you talking to me? Yes?"

The word "yes" echoed against the ruin walls.

"You probably want to buy my bull."

"Bul-l-l" echoed back.

"How much will you pay? Will you give me ten *dram*s?"*

"Ten *dra-a-am*s."

"Will you pay me right now or tomorrow?"

"Tomorrow-w-w."

"Very well, I'll come back tomorrow. I hope you'll have the money ready."

"Ready-y-y."

Deciding that the bargain was sealed, the foolish brother tethered the bull to the ruins and headed home whistling merrily.

The next day he awoke early and set out to collect his money. During the night wolves had torn the bull to pieces. When the foolish brother came to the spot where he had tethered the bull, he found only gnawed bones.

"This means that you slaughtered the bull and ate him. Is that right?"

"Righ-h-ht."

"Was he tasty or not?"

"Not-t-t."

"Of course, that doesn't concern me. You bought the bull from me, so you must pay me. Until you pay me, I won't leave."

"Leave-e-e."

When the foolish brother heard this word, he flew into a rage in earnest. He grabbed a thick stick and began beating the ancient ruins. Several stones fell to the ground. It so happened that long ago someone had hidden a treasure in the ancient walls. When the stones fell, golden coins scattered in a heap at the fool's feet.

"Excellent," exclaimed the fool. "Only what will I do with all this money? You owe me only ten *dram*s, so I'll take only the money you owe me and leave the rest to you."

He took one gold coin and returned home.

"Well, did you sell your bull?" asked the clever brother, smiling all the while.

"I did."

"Who bought it?"

"The ruins bought it."

"And did they pay you?"

"Of course. At first they tried not to pay me. But I beat them with a stick, and they showed me all their money. I took only one gold coin in payment for their debt. I left the rest of the money where it lay." The fool took a gold coin out of his pocket and showed it to his brother.

The clever brother's eyes grew round with astonishment. "Where is this place?" he asked.

"No, I won't tell you where it is. You're greedy. If I show you where it is, you'll take everything for yourself and you'll make me carry it home on my back."

The clever brother swore that he would carry the treasure home himself if only the foolish brother would show him where it was. "Give me your gold coin and lead me to the ruins. I'll buy you a new outfit."

When the fool heard that he would receive a new outfit, he immediately gave his brother the gold coin and led him to the ruins.

The clever brother brought all of the gold home and soon grew wealthy. However, he didn't buy his brother a new outfit as he had promised.

The foolish brother reminded the clever brother about his promise not once, not twice, but continually to no avail. Finally, he decided to go to court.

"Oh, judge," he said, pleading his case. "I had a bull, and I sold the bull to the ruins. . . ."

"That's enough!" the judge interrupted. "Where did this fool come from? So you 'sold the bull to the ruins'?" mimicked the judge. And he had the fool removed from court.

Then the foolish brother began complaining to others, but everyone laughed at him. It is said that to this day the fool wanders the world in rags complaining to one and all. But no one believes his story. They only laugh at him, and the clever brother laughs with them, too.

---

*The *dram* is Armenia's basic monetary unit.

SILLY PUGI AND THE EGG-HATCHING PERSIANS

Silly Pugi's* name is known throughout Armenia. It is well known in many countries that Silly Pugi is not only wise, but quick-witted. He's a practical joker with a sharp tongue.

Several rich men from Persia, who were also quick-witted and had sharp tongues, decided to visit *Melik*** Shakhnazar, Silly Pugi's master. "Let's go visit *Melik* Shakhnazar and see what Silly Pugi is like. Let's play a trick on him," they said.

After arriving in the town of Shush, where *Melik* Shakhnazar lived, the Persians began searching for the *melik*'s home.

Silly Pugi observed the visitors approaching from afar. He ran into *Melik* Shakhnazar's yard and grabbed a wicker basket. He put several eggs into the basket. Then he threw some rags into the basket, sat on the eggs, and began clucking like a hen.

When the guests approached, they saw Silly Pugi and asked him, "What are you doing?"

"Don't talk to me. I'm hatching eggs. If I move, I'll break all the eggs."

"We've come to visit *Melik* Shakhnazar," the strangers announced, "but we don't know where his house is. Show us!"

"If the whole world went topsy-turvy, I wouldn't move from this spot because the eggs would break and they wouldn't hatch," answered Silly Pugi.

"But we have urgent business with *Melik* Shakhnazar," the strangers insisted. "Show us *Melik* Shakhnazar's house."

Silly Pugi grabbed one of the strangers by the hem of his robe and said, "Sit here in my place. Keep in mind that if I come back and see that you got up, it won't go well for you."

The stranger whom Silly Pugi had grabbed by the hem was horrified. However, after glancing around and noticing that no one was in the vicinity, he sat down on the eggs to hatch them.

Silly Pugi went off supposedly to search for *Melik* Shakhnazar.

After awaking from his nap, *Melik* Shakhnazar went out of his house and saw several strangers standing beside his door. One of them was in the yard sitting in a wicker basket.

Melik Shakhnazar descended the steps of his house and asked, "Who are you?"

"We came to visit *Melik* Shakhnazar."

"I am *Melik* Shakhnazar, and this is my home."

Then *Melik* Shakhnazar asked the Persian sitting in the basket, "What are you doing, stranger? Why are you sitting in a basket?"

"Be quiet," the stranger shushed him. "I must sit here until the eggs hatch or the owner of the basket returns."

"Who's that?" asked *Melik* Shakhnazar.

"It was a man."

Melik Shakhnazar bit his lip. He understood right away that Silly Pugi must have had something to do with it.

At that moment Silly Pugi appeared. As Silly Pugi approached, *Melik* Shakhnazar asked the strangers mockingly, "Why have you come?"

"We heard that a man by the name of Silly Pugi lives here and that he is a sharp-tongued practical joker. We came to play a trick on him."

"May your hearth be blessed," laughed *Melik* Shakhnazar. "You have not yet crossed the threshold of my home, and yet Silly Pugi has already played a trick on you. He has tricked you into sitting in a basket to hatch eggs, as if you were a hen."

Blushing with shame, the Persians turned around and went home without realizing their plan.

---

*Pronounced Póogee.

**There were five hereditary *melik*s, or rulers, one for each of Armenia'a five principalities in Karabakh.

THREE BROTHERS BRING A COMPLAINT TO SILLY PUGI

*P*eople came to *Melik* Shakhnazar from a neighboring village to lodge a complaint. "May you have a long life, *Melik*," said one of the complainants. "We are three brothers. Our father left us an inheritance that included seventeen camels. In his will he wrote that half of the camels were to be given to me since I am the oldest brother. A third of the camels belongs to my middle brother, and a ninth of them belongs to my youngest brother. We can't seem to divide the camels up as Father instructed, and because of this we quarreled. We haven't been able to find anyone who can arbitrate amongst us and divide our inheritance.

"I proposed selling all seventeen camels and then dividing the money as Father instructed, but my youngest brother isn't in agreement. Now we have come to you to request that you judge our case."

Melik Shakhnazar thought long and hard and came to understand that deciding this case was beyond his ability. Silly Pugi was needed here.

"What do you say, Pugi?" asked *Melik* Shakhnazar. "How can the seventeen camels be divided amongst three brothers?"

Silly Pugi knew that it was impossible to divide the camels as the brothers' father wanted. The number seventeen can't be divided by three, let alone by nine.

Finally, Silly Pugi said, "Very well, go back to your village. Tomorrow I'll come and divide the camels."

The next morning Silly Pugi mounted his camel and set out for the brothers' village. They were waiting impatiently for him.

"Where are your camels? Drive them here to me," commanded Silly Pugi.

The brothers rode up with their seventeen camels.

"Now drive my camel over to yours," ordered Silly Pugi.

"How many camels are there now?" he asked after the brothers had done as he ordered.

"Eighteen," the brothers answered in a single voice.

"Half of eighteen is nine. Nine camels go to the oldest brother. Are you satisfied?" asked Silly Pugi.

"We're satisfied," said the brothers.

"A third of eighteen is six. Isn't that right?" asked Silly Pugi.

"Right," the brothers affirmed.

"Six will go to the middle brother. Correct?"

"Correct," replied the brothers.

"A ninth of eighteen is two. True?" asked Silly Pugi.

"True," replied the brothers.

"Two camels are for the youngest brother. Are you satisfied?"

"We're satisfied," affirmed the brothers.

"One camel is left, and it is mine. Good luck!" said Silly Pugi. Then he mounted his camel and left.

SILLY PUGI AND HIS FRIEND

Silly Pugi took his friend hunting on the condition that if a bear attacked them, they would defend one another.

The friends came to the forest. From out of the blue a bear appeared and attacked the hunters. The bear barely grazed Silly Pugi with his paw, but Silly Pugi fell to the ground face down and held his breath, pretending to be dead.

The beast sniffed the hunter. Deciding that he was dead, the bear went away.

Silly Pugi's friend, after catching sight of the bear, had thrown down his rifle and had climbed a tree.

After the bear left, the friend climbed down and asked Silly Pugi, who was lying on the ground, "For goodness sake, what did the bear whisper to you?"

"The bear said, 'Let this incident be a lesson to you. In the future don't befriend a man who saves himself and leaves his friend in trouble.'"

SILLY PUGI AND THE TEACHER

*S*illy Pugi set out for his teacher's to learn reading and writing. The teacher gave his student a book and asked him to repeat what he said, word by word.

"Pugi, say 'A' (*aib*)."*

Pugi was silent.

"Pugi, say 'A' (*aib*)," repeated the teacher.

Pugi continued to be silent.

"Pugi, say 'A' (*aib*)," insisted the teacher.

But Pugi was stubbornly silent.

Pugi's fellow villagers began asking Pugi to repeat everything that the teacher said. "Why can't you say 'A' (*aib*)? Is that so difficult?" asked one of Pugi's acquaintances.

"Oh, you unfortunate wretch, is it really so difficult to say 'A' (*aib*)?" asked another villager.

"If I say 'A' (*aib*)," Pugi explained, "then I'll have to say 'B' (*ben*). If I say 'B' (*ben*), then I'll have to say 'C' (*gim*). I don't want to say 'A' so that the teacher will leave me in peace."

**Aib, *ben*, *gim* (A, B, C) are letters of the ancient Armenian alphabet.

PUGI AND HIS WIFE

*P*ugi was sleeping soundly, snoring away. His wife was rocking the baby in the cradle. Because of Pugi's snoring, the baby couldn't sleep and kept crying.

"Husband, husband, get up," said Silly Pugi's wife. "Get up and rock the cradle for a while. After all, half of the child is yours. I'm tired. I'm worn out," said Pugi's wife in an attempt to persuade her husband to help out.

Awaking, Pugi answered, "You rock your half of the baby while my half cries." Then, turning onto his right side, Pugi began snoring even louder.

THE RAVEN

One day Pugi caught a raven and brought it home.

"Why do you need a raven?" his amazed neighbors asked. "What use is it?"

"It is said that the raven lives for 200 years," answered Silly Pugi. "If it lives with me, I'll be able to find out whether or not it's true."

PUGI AND HIS NEIGHBOR

*O*ne day Pugi's neighbor came to see him. "Give me your donkey so that I can ride to the mill to get my grain ground."

"My dear man, I would give you the donkey gladly, but he's not at home," answered Pugi.

At that moment, the donkey began braying loudly in the barn.

"And you have the nerve to say that the donkey's not at home!" said the indignant neighbor when he heard the braying donkey.

"Hey, you are an amazing man," answered Pugi. "You don't believe me, but you believe my donkey."

APPENDIX A:
ARMENIAN CUISINE

Armenians are known for their hospitality and sociability, so entertaining guests is an important part of Armenian life. A courteous guest never refuses to taste what is offered at the Armenian table. Entertaining guests is so important to the Armenians that there was even an ancient god of hospitality and plenty, named Vanatur. Vanatur's feast day used to be celebrated during harvest time on August 11, the first day of the ancient Armenian New Year.

Armenian cuisine is one of the oldest in the world. After all, Armenia is considered by some to be the cradle of civilization and the location of the biblical Noah's ark.

Over the years Armenian cuisine has been influenced by the cuisines of many other nations. Invaders and conquerors left their mark. Among them were Assyrians, Persians, Greeks, Romans, Arabs, Egyptians, Mongols, Iranians, Russians, and Turks. Armenia had contact with its neighbors, too. The influences of Georgia, Azerbaijan, and Syria are apparent in Armenian cuisine. The Diaspora added more variety to Armenian food. Often there is a hint of America, France, Australia, and the Middle East in Armenian cuisine. Because of similarities with dishes of many countries, Armenia's cuisine might be called multi-ethnic.

Armenian cooking is distinguished by the use of the *tonir*, an underground ceramic oven. Flat breads and meat dishes are prepared in this special oven.

Vegetables are an important component of the Armenian diet because there are more than 180 fast days in the Church calendar on which meat and dairy cannot be eaten. Therefore, Armenians have learned to like vegetables, grains, and beans, which serve as substitutes for forbidden fare.

Daily meals consist of breakfast (*entrik*), lunch (*nakhajash*), dinner (*jash*), and a light late meal, which is also called *entrik*. Dinner is served from 5:00 P.M. to 7:00 P.M. and constitutes a full-course meal. A typical dinner consists of an appetizer, soup, the main course, dessert, and beverages.*

Possible appetizers include meat jerky (*basturma*), paté of red beans and walnuts, cheese, and vegetable salads. Appetizers that indicate a Russian influence include smoked salmon, salted fish, caviar, and julienne mushrooms. There are those, like food and wine critic Hrayr Berberoglu, who believe that the Russian influence on Armenian cuisine has

---

ruined rather than enriched it, but nevertheless that influence has been present since Soviet days.** The entire array of tempting dishes is topped off with the ubiquitous flat bread.

The second course is soup. Lavash soup (*t'ghit*), meatball soup (*kufta*), traditional ham hock soup (*khash*), or yogurt soup (*spas*) might be served. Or, once again, a Russian influence might surface in a beet soup (*borscht*) or cold cucumber kvass soup (*okroshka*).

Possibilities for the main course include meat and rice wrapped in cabbage leaves or stuffed into vegetables (*dolma*); shashlik or shish kebab of lamb, chicken, beef, or pork (*khorovats*); balls of meat served with melted butter (*kufta*); and lamb or mutton. Grilled vegetables and a pilaf might accompany the meat.

The dessert is certain to include fruit. Other possibilities are phyllo pastry with honey and nuts (*pakhlava*), cake, ice cream, and honey and nuts in shredded wheat (*kataifi*). A candy made of sesame seed paste, fruit, and nuts (*halvah*) and a small cup of strong Armenian coffee, which is stronger than expresso, might top off the meal, along with some quality cognac, for which Armenia is famed.

A glance at the typical menus above reveals the staples of Armenian cuisine. The importance of breads, which are served with every meal, cannot be overemphasized. The favorite is the thin flat bread called *lavash*.

Grains, which have been grown in Armenia since ancient times, are used in making bread, pilaf, and *dolma*. Wheat, cultivated by the Hittites long before Christ's birth, is perhaps the most important grain and is available in various forms. It is used in soups as whole kernels and in boiled, ground, hulled, and dry forms. The most popular is bulgur (cracked wheat). Other grains used include rice, millet, and barley.

Dairy products include a homemade yogurt called *mazdoon*, cheese, and buttermilk.

Another staple in the Armenian diet is beans. Lentils, string beans, and peas are frequently combined in Armenian dishes.

Meats include the preferred lamb, traditionally preserved in its fat, which is cut off as needed. Since lamb is expensive, wheat is often added to extend it. Other meats are pork, chicken, and beef. Fish is prepared less often, but lake trout is quite popular.

The favorite vegetable is probably eggplant. Others include onions, green beans, cucumbers, tomatoes, okra, peppers (especially the Aleppo pepper), squash, garlic, carrots, and mushrooms. Vegetables are prepared roasted, raw, stewed, marinated, dried, and pickled.

The variety of fruit available in Armenia is staggering. There are pomegranates, figs, apricots, grapes, plums, pears, apples, raisins, lemons, peaches, and quince. Quince is a hard, sour fruit that is used in meat dishes to create a unique flavor.

Nuts are also part of Armenian cuisine. The walnut is native to Armenia and makes an appearance in many dishes. Almonds and hazelnuts are used, too.

Vegetable oils are not popular, with the exception of sunflower oil, which is again indicative of a Russian influence. Butter and olive oil are the oils of preference.

Spices are varied and abundant. Among them are garlic, basil, coriander, rosemary, thyme, cilantro, parsley, mint, cumin, tarragon, saffron, and paprika. Vanilla, rose water, cinnamon, and cardamom are used, too. A *bouquet garni* of pepper, paprika, fenugreek, dill, cumin, clove, sage, allspice, and nutmeg is used. The blend is called *chaimen*. Some dishes call for a Turkish Armenian spice called *mahleb*, ground pits of black cherries.

Following are recipes for some of Armenia's traditional dishes, which are both tasty and healthy.

---

* For a description of possible meals and food combinations, see *Tour Armenia: About Armenian Food*. Available at http://www.tacentral.com/dining.asp (accessed March 19, 2006), from which the examples here were selected.

** *Food for Thought: Armenian Cuisine Then and Now*. Available at http://www.jewelsoffood. com/index.cfm?fuseaction=writings.articl... (accessed March 19, 2006).

Stuffed Vegetables (*Dolmas*)

Vegetables stuffed with rice and ground meat are called *dolmas*. Easy to prepare, this traditional meal is served frequently in Armenian families.

Ingredients:

1 slender eggplant

1 green pepper

1 summer squash or zucchini

1 tomato

1 14.5 oz. can diced tomatoes

Filling

½ lb. ground lamb

½ cup bulgur (cracked wheat)

1 onion

1 slivered garlic clove

1 cup chopped fresh parsley

½ tsp. dill

1 tbsp. chopped fresh mint

salt and pepper to taste

Directions:

1. Cut eggplant and summer squash in half. Cut off top of pepper and tomato. Remove and discard vegetable seeds. Lightly salt inside of vegetables.

---

2. Mix filling with half can of diced tomatoes, and stuff the vegetables. Put top on pepper and tomato. Arrange vegetables in a baking pan. Pour remainder of diced tomatoes over top of vegetables.

3. Cover the baking pan and bake in a slow oven at 325° Fahrenheit (161° Celsius) for 1 hour and 15 minutes.

Armenian Pilaf

Armenian pilaf is distinguished by the addition of thin spaghetti to the rice. This mixture makes a delicious dish.

Ingredients:

¼ stick butter

2 tbsp. olive oil

1 onion

½ cup thin spaghetti broken into small pieces

1 cup long-grain rice

2½ cups chicken broth

salt and pepper to taste

Directions:

1. Sauté thin spaghetti in olive oil and butter until brown. Add onion and sauté until translucent. Add long-grain rice and stir until coated. Add broth and seasoning. Let simmer for 25 minutes.

2. When the broth is no longer visible, the pilaf is done. Turn off the heat and let sit for 7 minutes. Fluff pilaf and serve.

Chicken Shish Kebab or Shashlik (*Khorovats*)

Kebabs are made of pork, chicken, lamb, and beef. The most common kebabs are lamb and pork, but chicken is delicious, too.

Ingredients:

2 lbs. boned chicken

Marinade

2 slivered garlic cloves

4 tbsp. lemon juice

salt and pepper to taste

4 tbsp. olive oil

1 tsp. dried mint

Directions:

1. Cut the chicken into chunks. Mix ingredients for marinade sauce. Add chunks of chicken to marinade, stir, and cover. Place in refrigerator for at least 3 hours.

2. Remove from refrigerator and thread onto skewers. Broil or cook on an outside grill until done. Turn at least once. Serve with pilaf.

Roast Leg of Lamb

Ingredients:

1 6-lb. leg of lamb

1 tsp. dried mint

1 tsp. dried rosemary or fresh branch

1 onion, sliced

1 slivered garlic clove

salt and pepper to taste

Directions:

1. Heat oven to 375° Fahrenheit (188° Celsius). Salt and pepper leg of lamb. Place leg in a roasting pan with the fat side up. Sprinkle seasonings on the lamb. If you choose to use fresh rosemary, place a branch on top of the leg. Place onion slices and garlic slivers on top of the leg. Roast for 2 hours.

2. Remove roast when done and let it sit for 7 minutes.

3. Water and flour can be added to the drippings to make gravy. Stir on low heat until the mixture thickens.

String Beans and Tomato

Ingredients:

1 lb. string beans

1 onion

1 slivered garlic clove

1 14.5 oz. can diced tomatoes

4 tbsp. olive oil

water or lamb broth

parsley, basil, mint to taste

salt and pepper to taste

Directions:

1. Cut string beans on the bias. Set aside.
2. Chop onion and sauté with minced garlic and olive oil until translucent. Add canned diced tomatoes. Simmer.
3. Add string beans and seasonings. Cover with water or lamb broth. Simmer until beans are cooked, about 10 to 12 minutes.

Dry Bean *Plaki*

Ingredients:

1½ cups dried northern beans

6½ cups water

4 carrots (scraped and cubed)

1 green pepper

¼ cup chopped celery

¼ cup fresh chopped parsley

3 peeled and slivered garlic cloves

salt and pepper to taste

1 14.5 oz. can diced tomatoes

½ cup olive oil

Directions:

1. Wash beans and cook in water over moderate heat 1½ hours.
2. Add carrots, green pepper, celery, parsley, garlic, salt, and pepper, and cook an additional 30 minutes. Add tomatoes.
3. Cover and cook 15 minutes longer, until beans are soft. Before cooking time is over, add olive oil and cook 15 minutes more. Serve hot or cold.

Yogurt (*Madzoon*)

Madzoon is healthy homemade yogurt, which figures importantly in the diet of the people living in the Caucasus, the home of some of the world's oldest inhabitants. A yogurt starter that contains live bacteria, from which batch after batch of *madzoon* is made, is kept in Armenian households. Plain yogurt with live cultures that can be used as a starter can also be found in health food stores.

Ingredients:

1 quart unpasteurized whole milk, if possible

¼ cup yogurt starter with live cultures

Directions:

1. Pour milk into clean pot. Bring to a boil. Transfer liquid to a glass container and let it cool.
2. Stir the starter with a small amount of warm milk in another bowl. Pour the mixture into the glass bowl with the rest of the milk. Stir. Cover the glass bowl with a towel.
3. Let the mixture sit in a warm place for at least 6 hours.
4. Refrigerate and serve.

Yogurt Drink (*Tahn*)

Tahn is a cold drink served with meals that is especially popular on warm days.

Ingredients:

1 cup cold yogurt

1 cup cold water or seltzer water

pinch of salt

ice cubes

sprig of mint

Directions:

1. Pour yogurt, water, and salt into a bowl or blender.
2. Mix well. Serve over ice cubes with a sprig of mint.

String Cheese

String cheese is an entertaining food because the stretching process required to make it is fun for everyone.

Ingredients:

½ lb. mozzarella or other white cheese

¼ cup water

pinch of *mahleb* (ground black cherry pits; can be obtained in Middle Eastern markets)

Directions:

1. Bring cheese and water to a boil in a saucepan. Add a pinch of *mahleb*. Cook until cheese is melted and there are no lumps. Drain excess water and let cool until cheese can be handled.
2. Pull cheese into a foot-long strand. Fold in half, pinch together, and stretch twice more.
3. Twist into a braid by twisting each end in opposite directions. Wrap in plastic and refrigerate.

Fruit Compote (*Khoshab*)

Ingredients:

1 cup dried apricots

1 cup dried prunes

1 cup dried figs

(A package of mixed dried fruit may be substituted for the apricots, figs, and prunes.)

½ cup raisins

cinnamon stick

¼ cup honey

1 tbsp. lemon juice

2½ cups boiling water

Directions:

1. Dice the apricots, prunes, and figs. Heat them along with raisins in the water to the boiling point.
2. Add cinnamon stick. Simmer for 15 to 20 minutes.
3. Add honey and lemon juice. Cool and refrigerate.

Baklava (*Pakhlava*)

Baklava is an ancient dish that is thought to have originated with the Assyrians. Each culture has developed its own variation of the original. The Greeks make baklava with honey so that the dessert is very sweet. Arabs make a lighter version with rose water. The Armenians make their own version with cinnamon and cloves.*

Ingredients:

2 sticks unsalted butter

18 sheets phyllo dough, thawed, if previously frozen

2 cups chopped walnuts

pinch cinnamon

2 tbsp. sugar

Syrup

1½ cups sugar

½ cup honey

3 tbsp. lemon juice

1 cup water

1 whole clove

Directions:

1. To make syrup, boil water, sugar, clove, and honey. Turn down heat and simmer until mixture thickens. Remove from heat. Remove clove and add lemon juice. Cool.

2. Mix walnuts, cinnamon, and 2 tbsp. sugar in bowl. Set aside.

3. Melt butter. Brush a baking pan with butter. Put 2 phyllo sheets into pan and brush with melted butter. Repeat twice until there are 6 layers. Spread walnut filling over 6th layer. Repeat the process twice until the pan contains 18 layers.

4. Refrigerate pan for 45 minutes. Remove and cut into 2- to 3-inch squares or diamond shapes.

5. Preheat oven to 350° Fahrenheit (175° Celsius). Bake for 30 to 40 minutes. Pour warm syrup over browned top, and cool to room temperature.

---

* For a brief history of baklava, see *Wikipedia: Baklava*. Available at http://en.wikipedia.org/wiki/Baklava (accessed March 19, 2006).

APPENDIX B: GLOSSARY

aga: Muslim title of respect.

Amanor: New Year. Secular holiday observed on January 1.

Ar: Armenian sun god.

Aragats, Mount: Highest mountain in present-day Armenia and fourth highest mountain of the Armenian highlands. It is an extinct volcano located about 25 miles (40 kilometers) northwest of the capital, Yerevan. Also known as Mount Alagez.

Araks River: River that flows through eastern Turkey to the Caspian Sea.

Ararat, Mount: Mountain once located in Armenia and now in eastern Turkey. Known to Armenians as Masis. In Armenian tradition, Noah's ark landed on Mount Ararat after the flood. Prior to that, the mountain was regarded as the home of Armenia's pagan gods. Therefore, Mount Ararat is closely linked to the Armenian sense of identity.

arisa: Dish prepared with chicken and wheat.

ashug: Folksinger; minstrel who composes and performs songs.

Astghik: Armenian goddess of love.

azan: Muslim summons to prayer, called by the *muezzin* (crier) from the minaret of a mosque five times daily.

Azeris: Shiite Muslim people of Azerbaijan and Iran.

Baku: Oil-rich capital of Azerbaijan and largest city on the Caspian Sea.

balik-dzhan: Little child; dear soul.

borscht: Beet soup.

bulgur: Cracked wheat.

chaimen: *Bouquet garni* of pepper, paprika, fenugreek, allspice, dill, cumin, clove, nutmeg, and sage.

choereg: Sweet bread baked at Easter.

---

cornel tree: Tree of the dogwood family, with very hard wood, edible fruit, and small, perfect flowers; related to the cherry tree.

couch grass: Prolific European grass. The American version is a tenacious weed known as quack grass.

dervish: Muslim dedicated to a life of poverty and chastity. Some whirl and chant as part of their religious ritual.

dev: Variously interpreted to be a monster, dragon, serpent, or giant. In Armenian mythology, immortal spirits who inhabit old ruins. Some are good, such as Aralez, who licks the wounds of warriors fallen in battle. Others, such as the dragon Vishap, are evil.

dhol: Drum.

dolma: Cabbage leaves, grape leaves, and vegetables stuffed with meat and rice.

dram: Basic Armenian monetary unit, composed of 100 small coins called *lumma*s. Derived from the Greek word *drachma*, the modern *dram* was introduced on November 22, 1993.

dzhan: Title of respect indicating "dear life" or "dear soul."

Dzmer Papik: Armenian Santa Claus.

entrik: Breakfast and light supper.

fez: Flat, brimless hat worn in the Near East.

Frangistan: Western Europe. Also spelled Farengstan or Frankistan.

halvah: Candy made with sesame seeds, fruit, nuts, and honey.

hekiat: Armenian word for "folktale."

Hodja: Title of respect; also, master or teacher.

Ispagan: City located in Persia, present-day Iran. Alternative spellings include Isfagan and Isfahan.

jash: Dinner.

kataifi: Shredded wheat with honey and nuts.

khash: Ham hock soup.

khorovats: Shashlik; skewered kebabs of meat. Also spelled *khorovadz*.

khoshab: Fruit compote.

kufta: Meatball soup.

last: Wooden block on which a shoe is repaired.

lavash: Flat bread.

lumma: Small coin; 100 *lumma*s constitute a *dram*, Armenia's basic monetary unit.

madzoon: Sour milk, yogurt.

mahleb: Spice composed of ground black cherry pits.

märchen: German word for "fairy tales."

melik: Prince; one of five hereditary rulers of five Armenian principalities in Karabakh—Dizak, Giulistan, Khachen, Dzharaberd, and Varanda. They took care of judicial and military business.

nakhajash: Lunch.

nakharas: Native Armenian princes chosen to rule by the Persians of the Sassanid Dynasty.

Nani-dzhan: Mother—dear soul.

nazir: Government official.

okroshka: Cold cucumber kvass soup.

pakhlava: Baklava.

palan: Felt saddle for pack animals.

peri: In ancient Persian mythology, a spirit descended from fallen angels and not permitted into paradise without doing penance. More recently, thought to be a beautiful, benevolent fairy. In Greek mythology, an oread, or nymph, of mountains and caves.

plaki: Dish cooked with olive oil and vegetables.

pourquoi tales: Tales that explain how something originated or acquired its characteristics; explanatory tales. *Pourquoi* is French for "why."

saz: Small mandolin with a long neck used by *ashugs*, or minstrels, to accompany their songs.

spas: Yogurt soup.

Sumgait: Third largest city in Azerbaijan; located on the shore of the Caspian Sea. Site of the February 1988 massacre of ethnic Armenians by Azeri Turks in a dispute over the control of Nagorno-Karabakh.

tahn: Cold yogurt drink.

t'ghit: Lavash soup.

tonir: Stove or oven set in the ground with clay walls for the purpose of baking bread.

Trndez: Purification, observed on February 14 to mark forty days after Christ's birth and to celebrate the coming of spring.

Tsaghkazard: Palm Sunday, the observance of Christ's coming to Jerusalem as the Savior.

Vanatur: Pagan god of hospitality and plenty.

Vardanants: Day commemorating the memory of Vardan Mamikonian (AD 400–451) for defending the Christians against the Persian Zoroastrians. Observed the Thursday preceding Lent.

Vardavar: Transfiguration and summer holiday during which the pagan Astghik, goddess of love, is honored.

Vishap: Mythical dragon, winged snake, or snake-like fish; evil thunder spirit that tramples crops. Associated with Vahagn, the god of thunder and lightning. Dragon stones, fish-like carvings in stone, are found in Armenia.

Vishapakagh: Dragon slayer; dragon-rug.

vizier: High officer, or minister of state, in the Ottoman Empire, who takes on duties for the ruler.

Yerevan: Capital of Armenia. Founded in 782 BC by King Argishti during the time of the Urartu kingdom.

Zatik: Easter, the favorite holiday of Armenians.

zurna: Loud wooden wind musical instrument that sounds similar to the clarinet or bugle. Traditionally played at weddings and festivals.

BIBLIOGRAPHY

Folktales: Books and Periodicals

Armenian Folk Tales. Translated from Armenian into Russian by I. Khatchatrianz. Translated into English by N. W. Orloff. Philadelphia: Colonial House, 1946.

Bogoliubskaia, M. K., and A. L. Tabenkina, comps. *Khrestomatiia po detskoi literature: Uchebnoe posobie dlia doshkol'nykh pedagogicheskikh uchilishch*. 5th ed. Moscow: Prosveshchenie, 1968.

———. *Nashi skazki: Skazki, i pesenki narodov SSSR*. Vol. 2. Bibliotechka detskogo sada. Moscow: Detskaia literatura, 1966.

Downing, Charles, trans. *Armenian Folk-tales and Fables*. Oxford, New York, Toronto: Oxford University Press, 1972.

Fedorenko, P. K., comp. *Bol'shaia khrestomatiia liubimykh skazok*. Moscow: Planeta detstva, 2001.

Goretskii, V. G., et al., comps. *Kniga dlia chteniia: Uchebnik dlia uchashchikhsia 3 klassa trekhletnei nachal'noi shkoly*. Vol. 1. Moscow: Prosveshchenie, 1990.

Grinblat, M. Ia., and A. I. Gurskii, comps. *Skazki narodov SSSR*. Minsk: Narodnaia asveta, 1970.

Hoogasian-Villa, Suzie, ed. and coll. *100 Armenian Tales and Their Folkloristic Relevance*. Detroit: Wayne State University Press, 1966.

Ioannisian, A. I., comp. *Armianskie skazki: Skazki araratskoi doliny*. Moscow: Khudozhestvennaia literatura, 1968.

Karapetian, G. O., trans. and comp. *Armianskii fol'klor*. Moscow: Nauka (Glavnaia redaktsiia vostochnoi literatury), 1979.

———. *Zabavnye i nazidatel'nye istorii armianskogo naroda*. Moscow: Nauka, 1975.

Khatchatrianz, I. *Armianskie skazki*. 2d ed. Moscow: Akademiia, 1933.

Murzilka 4, no. 4 (1973): 12.

Surmelian, Leon. *Apples of Immortality: Folktales of Armenia*. Berkeley and Los Angeles: University of California Press, 1968.

Tashjian, Virginia A. *Once There Was and Was Not: Armenian Tales Retold*. Boston: Little, Brown, 1966.

————. *Three Apples Fell from Heaven: Armenian Folk Tales Retold*. Boston: Little, Brown, 1971.

Folktales: Web Sites

Armenian Fairy Tales "Hekiats." Available: http://www.armenianheritage.com/lafairy.htm. (Accessed February 3, 2005).

Kids: Armenian Fairy Tales. Available: http://www.armeniaemb.org/Kids/ArmenianFairyTales/Index.htm. (Accessed January 23, 2005).

Kollektsiia armianskogo fol'klora: Pritchi. Available: http://www.armeniantales.narod.ru/pritchi.htm. (Accessed April 30, 2005).

Kollektsiia armianskogo fol'klora: Skazki i predaniia. Available: http://www.armeniantales.narod.ru/skazki.htm. (Accessed April 30, 2005).

Skazki narodov mira: Armianskie skazki. Available: http://www.skazka.com.ru/people/arm/arm.html. (Accessed August 12, 2005).

Your Gateway to Armenia Online: Armenian Stories. Available: http://www.parev.net/armenian-stories.htm. (Accessed February 3, 2005).

Cuisine: Books

Ghazarian, Barbara. *Simply Armenian: Naturally Healthy Ethnic Cooking Made Easy*. Monterey, CA: Mayreni Publishing, 2004.

Manoogian, Mrs. Alex, ed. *Treasured Armenian Recipes*. New York: The Detroit Women's Chapter of AGBU, 1949; Southfield, MI: The Detroit Women's Chapter of AGBU, 1980.

Saint George Maronite Catholic Church. *Lebanese and Middle Eastern Recipe Favorites*. Portsmouth, NH: Little Flower Publications, 1998.

Uvezian, Sonia. *The Cuisine of Armenia*. New York: Hippocrene, 1974.

Vassilian, Hamo, ed. *Ethnic Cookbooks and Food Marketplace: A Complete Bibliographic Guide and Directory to Armenian, Iranian, Afghan, Middle Eastern, North African and Greek Foods in the USA and Canada*. Glendale, CA: Armenian Reference Books, 1991.

Wise, Victoria Jenanyan. *The Armenian Table: More than 165 Treasured Recipes That Bring Together Ancient Flavors and 21st-Century Style*. New York: St. Martin's Press, 2004.

Cuisine: Web Sites

Adventures in Armenian Cooking. Available: http://www.saintsarkis.org/laydies_guild_cookbook.htm. (Accessed January 21, 2006).

Armenia Fest: Foods and Delicacies. Available: http://www.armeniafest.com/foods/recipes2.html. (Accessed March 25, 2006).

Armeniapedia, The Armenia Encyclopedia: Adventures in Armenian Cooking. Available: http://www.armeniapedia.org/index.php?=Adventures_in_Armenia (Accessed April 8, 2006).

Astray Recipes. Available: http://www.astray.com/recipes/. (Accessed March 19, 2006).

Chef Moz Dining Guide. Available: http://www.chefmoz.org/Armenia/. (Accessed April 8, 2006).

Chefs: Feed Your Passion. Available: http://www.chefs.com. (Accessed June 1, 2006).

Food Down Under: Armenian. Available: http://fooddownunder.com/cgi-bin/search.cgi?q=armenian. (Accessed April 9, 2006).

The Gutsy Gourmet: Dining at Noah's Table, Cuisine of Ancient Armenia. Available: http://www.thegutsygourmet.net/armenian.html. (Accessed January 23, 2006).

Hamerkaz Online. Available: http://www.hamerkaz.com.au/cooking.asp. (Accessed March 26, 2006).

Let's Eat—A Writer's Guide to Cooking. Available: http://www.williammichaelian.com/letseat/letseat.html. (Accessed March 27, 2006).

Madzoon. Available: http://www.georgefamily.net/cookbook/17Madzoon.html. (Accessed March 25, 2006).

MealMaster: String Cheese. Available: http://www.recipesource.com/text/ethnic/africa/middle-east/armenian/. (Accessed March 25, 2006).

Middle Eastern recipes: Khoshaf. Available: http://www.recipegoldmine.com/worldmideast/mideast12.html. (Accessed March 25, 2006).

Nina Lamb's Recipes and Food Memoirs. Available: http://www.ninalamb.com. (Accessed March 25, 2006).

Ohan Armoudian Creation-Recipes. Available: http://ohan.itlnet/personpages/recipes.htm (Accessed January 21, 2006).

Our Cookbook: Recipes from Armenia and around the World. Available: http://cookbook.armenians.com/ (Accessed April 8, 2006).

Welcome to the Egyptian Recipes Page: Koshaf. Available: http://www.touregypt.net/recipes/koshaf.htm. (Accessed March 25, 2006).

Wikipedia: Baklava. Available: http://en.wikipedia.org/wiki/Baklava. (Accessed March 19, 2006).

Maps: Books

Gilbert, Martin. *Atlas of Russian History*. New York: Dorset Press, 1985.

Grosvenor, Gilbert M., ed. *Peoples of the Soviet Union*. Cartographers William T. Peele and David W. Cook. Map Supplement to *National Geographic* 149, no. 2 (February 1976): 144A.

Mesiatseva, L. N., and L. A. Polianskaia, eds. *Malyi Atlas SSSR*. Moscow: Glavnoe upravlenie geodezii i kartografii pri sovete ministrov SSSR, 1973.

Maps: Web Sites

About. Geography: Armenia. Available: http://geography.about.com/library/maps/blarmenia.htm. (Accessed April 5, 2006). Student friendly site offers maps from *Merriam-Webster's Atlas*, a relief map, and a free blank map, as well as facts about Armenia.

Armenia: Holt, Rinehart, and Winston. Available: http://go.hrw.com/atlas/norm_htm/armenia.htm. (Accessed April 5, 2006).

Mapquest: Armenia. Available: http://www.mapquest.com/atlas/?region=armenia. (Accessed June 25, 2006).

Perry Castañeda Library Map Collection (Russia and the Former Soviet Republics Maps): The University of Texas at Austin. Available: http://www.lib.utexas.edu/maps/commonwealth.html. (Accessed June 25, 2006).

Quick Maps: Armenia. Available: http://www.theodora.com/maps/armenia_map.html. (Accessed June 25, 2006).

RECOMMENDED READINGS

History, Culture, and Travel

Agathangelos. *History of the Armenians*. Translated and with commentary by R. W. Thomson. Albany: State University of New York Press, 1976.

Apkarian-Russell, Pamela. *The Armenians of Worcester*. Portsmouth, NH: Arcadia Publishing, 2000.

"Armenian Americans." *Cobblestone: Discover American History* 21, no. 5 (May 2000): entire issue.

Avakian, Lindy V. *The Cross and the Crescent*. 3d ed. Phoenix: Golden West Publishers Unlimited, 1998.

Bagdasarian, Adam. *Forgotten Fire*. New York: Darling Kindersley Publishing, 2000.

Bakalian, Amy. "The Armenian Family and Related Topics: A Bibliography." *Armenian Review* 38, no. 4 (1985): 23–40.

Balakian, Peter. *The Burning Tigris: The Armenian Genocide and America's Response*. New York: HarperCollins, 2003.

Bamberger, Joan. "Family and Kinship in an Armenian-American Community." *Journal of Armenian Studies* 3 (1986–1987): 77–86.

Bardakjian, Kevork B. *A Reference Guide to Modern Armenian Literature 1500–1920*. Detroit: Wayne State University, 2000.

Bedickian, S. V. "How the Armenians Keep the New Year and Christmas." *Armenia* 3, no. 2 (1906): 8–12.

Bournoutian, George A. *A History of the Armenian People*. Costa Mesa, CA: Mazda Publishers, 1993.

Bulbulian, Berge. *The Fresno Armenians: History of a Diaspora Community*. Fresno: California State University Press, 2000.

Conybeare, Frederick Cornwallis. *The Armenian Church: Heritage and Identity*. New York: St. Vartan Press, 2001.

Dadrian, Vahakn N. *The History of the Armenian Genocide: Ethnic Conflict from the Balkans to Anatolia to the Caucasus*. Oxford and New York: Berghahn Books, 1995.

Davenport, Martha. "Armenian Embroidery in America." *Needle Arts* 12, no. 4 (1981): 16–17.

Der Manuelian, L., and M. B. Eiland. *Weavers, Merchants, and Rugs: The Inscribed Rugs of Armenia*. Fort Worth, TX: Kimball Art Museum, 1984.

Hewsen, Robert H. *Armenia: A Historical Atlas*. Chicago: University of Chicago Press, 2001.

Hovannisian, Richard G. *The Armenian Genocide: History, Politics, Ethics*. New York: St. Martin's Press, 1992.

Hovannisian, Richard G., ed. *The Armenian People from Ancient to Modern Times*. New York: Macmillan, 1997.

Johnson, Jerry L. *Crossing Borders—Confronting History: Intercultural Adjustment in a Post-Cold War World*. Lanham, MD: University Press of America, 1999.

Karanian, Matthew, and Robert Kurkjian. *Edge of Time: Traveling in Armenia and Karabagh*. 2d rev. ed. Northridge, CA: Stone Garden Productions, 2002.

Ketchum, Robert, Matthew Karanian, and Robert Kurkjian. *The Stone Garden Guide: Armenia and Karabagh*. Northridge, CA: Stone Garden Productions, 2004.

Koushagian, Torkom. *Saints and Feasts of the Armenian Church*. Translated and edited by Haigazoun Melkonian. New York: St. Vartan Press, 1988.

Kurdian, H. "A Historical Glimpse of the Art of Rug Weaving in Armenia." *Armenian Review* 1, no. 4 (1948): 22–30.

Marcom, Micheline Aharonian. *Three Apples Fell from Heaven*. New York: Riverhead, 2001.

Marshall, Annie C. "Armenian Industries." *Armenia* 4, no. 5 (1910): 5.

Matossian, Mary Kilbourne. "Armenian Society." *Armenian Review* 9, no. 3 (1956): 49–63.

Mazian, Florence. "Armenian Wedding Customs 1914: From Sacred to Profane." *Armenian Review* 37, no. 4 (1984): 1–13.

———. "The Patriarchal Armenian Family System." *Armenian Review* 36, no. 5 (1983): 14–26.

Moses of Khoren. *History of the Armenians*. Translated and with commentary by Robert W. Thomson. Harvard Armenian Texts and Studies, 4. Cambridge, MA: Harvard University Press, 1978.

Raphaelian, H. M. *Rugs of Armenia, Their History and Art*. New Rochelle, NY: Anatol Sivas, 1960.

Redgate, A. E. *The Armenians*. Oxford, England, and Malden, MA: Blackwell Publishing, 1998.

Russell, James R. *Zoroastrianism in Armenia*. Harvard Iranian Series, 5. Cambridge, MA: Harvard University, 1987.

Suny, Ronald Grigor. *Looking toward Ararat: Armenia in Modern History*. Bloomington: Indiana University Press, 1993.

Terjimanian, Hagop. *Armenian Holidays: Feasts and Holidays of the Armenian People*. Los Angeles: Abril, 1996.

Folklore and Mythology*

Ananikian, Mardiros H. "Armenian Mythology." In *The Mythology of All Races*. New York: Cooper Square Publishers, 1964.

Arvanian, Veronica. "The Living Cult of the Great Mother Anahit." *Armenian Review* 7, no. 2 (1954): 25–32.

Avakian, Anne M. "Three Apples Fell from Heaven." *Folklore* 98 (1987): 95–98.

Boettiger, Louis A. *Armenian Legends and Festivals*. Minnesota University Research Publications, Studies in the Social Sciences, 14. Minneapolis: University of Minnesota, 1920.

Garegin, Archbishop of Trebizond. "The Ancient Religion of the Armenians." *Armenian Review* 13, no. 2 (1960): 110–12.

Hazarabedian, Margit Abeghian. "A Bibliography of Armenian Folklore." *Armenian Review* 39, no. 3 (1986): 32–54.

Hoogasian-Villa, Susie, and Mary K. Matossian. *Armenian Village Life before 1914*. Detroit: Wayne State University Press, 1982.

Kalbouss, George. "On 'Armenian Riddles' and Their Offspring 'Radio Erevan.' " *Slavic and East European Journal*, series 2, no. 21 (1977): 447–49.

Kharatian, Z. V. "Traditional Demonological Notions of the Armenians." *Soviet Anthropology and Archeology* 20, no. 2 (1981): 28–55.

Matossian, Mary Kilbourne. "Birds, Bees, and Barley: Pagan Origins of Armenian Spring Rituals." *Armenian Review* 32 (1974): 292–302.

Russell, James R. "The Rites of the Armenian Goddess." *Ararat* 31, no. 3 (1990): 21–24.

———. "Dragons in Armenia: Some Observations." *Journal of Armenian Studies* 5 (1990-1991): 3–12.

Samulian, G. "Totemism among the Armenians." *Armenian Review* 2, no. 4 (1949): 54–64.

Wingate, J. S. "Armenian Folk-Tales." *Folk-Lore* 21 (1910): 217–22.

---

*An excellent selection of resources may be found in Anne M. Avakian's *Armenian Folklore Bibliography*. University of California Publications: Catalogs and Bibliographies, 11. Berkeley, Los Angeles, and London: University of California Press, 1994. Many of the citations listed here are also in her bibliography.

Folktales

Bider, Djemma. *A Drop of Honey: An Armenian Fable*. New York: Simon & Schuster, 1989.

Boyajian, Zabelle C. *Armenian Legends and Poems*. London: J. M. Dent, 1916. Reprint, New York: Columbia University Press, 1959.

Kudian, Mischa. *More Apples Fell from Heaven: A Selection of Armenian Folk and Fairy Tales*. London: Mashtots Press, 1983.

————. *Three Apples Fell from Heaven: A Collection of Armenian Folk and Fairy Tales*. London: Rupert Hart-Davis, 1969.

Lang, Andrew. *Olive Fairy Book*. New York: David McKay, 1950.

Russell, James R. "Armenian Tales." *Ararat* 28 (1987): 21–22.

Seklemian, A. G. "Armenian Fairy Tales." *Journal of American Folklore* 6 (1893): 150–52.

————. *The Golden Maiden and Other Folk Tales and Fairy Stories Told in Armenia*. Cleveland and New York: Holman-Taylor Co., 1898.

Servantsian, Karekin. "The Thousand-Throated Nightingale." Translated by J. G. Mandalian. *Armenian Review* 2 (1949): 152–54.

Tashjian, Virginia A. *The Miller King*. Boston: Ginn & Co., 1974.

Toumanian, Hovhannes. *Tales. Hovhannes Toumanian*. Yerevan, Armenia: Louys, 2002.

INDEX

Page numbers such as xxxiv n.28 refer to the page number and the numbered endnote in which that entry can be found (page xxxiv, note 28); page numbers such as 27 n refer to the unnumbered footnote on that page in which the entry is found (page 27, unnumbered note).

King of the Snakes. *See* "Peasant's Son and the King's Daughter, The"

King Turtamb. *See* "Dzheiran-ogly, the Deer's Son"

Kings. *See* Alexander the Great; "Beardless Sorcerer and the King's Son, The"; "Blacksmith, the Carpenter, and the Farmer, The"; "Forty Thieves"; "Gambar"; "Invincible Rooster, The"; Bagratuni I, King Gagik; Tigranes the Great; Tiridates (Trdat) III, King; "Little Bear"; "Ne'er-Do-Well Son, The"; "Peasant's Son and the King's Daughter, The"; "Pitcher of Gold, The"; "Snake Child Otsamanuk and Arevamanuk, Who Angered the Sun"; "The Tale about a Lazy Man, The"

King's daughter. *See* "Gambar"; "Little Bear"; "Peasant's Son and the King's Daughter, The"

King's son. *See* "Beardless Sorcerer and the King's Son, The"; "Dzheiran-ogly, the Deer's Son"; "Extraordinary Cucumber, The"; "Forty Thieves"; "Ne'er-Do-Well Son, The"

Kocharian, President Robert, xxi

"Know-It-All Tangik, xxxi, 112–13

Kotyak Region, *photo section*

Krag, Fire Spirit. *See* "Sun Maiden Arev and the Fire Spirit Krag, The"

Kurds, xvi

Lake Sevan, xvi

Lalayan, Ervand, xxvi

Lambs. *See* "Wolf and the Lamb, The"

Language, xviii–xix
    classical Armenian (Grabar), xviii
    dialects of tales, xxviii;
    Eastern Armenian, xviii
    Western Armenian, xviii

Lavash. See "Extraordinary Cucumber, The"

Laziness, xxxi. *See also* "Lazy Hoory"; "Lazy Tiuni and Uri the Slug"; "Tale about a Lazy Man, The"

"Lazy Hoory," xxxi, 128–30

"Lazy Tiuni and Uri the Slug," xxxi, 124–25

"Legend about Tiridates (Trdat) III, The," xvii, xxviii, xxix, 39–42

Legends. *See* Myths and legends

Lesser Armenia, xix, xx. *See also* Cilicia

Life, Armenian, xxii–xxiv
    family traditions, xxiv
    holidays, xxii–xxiv
    hospitality, xxii
    marriage, xxiv

"Little Bear," xxvii, xxviii, xxx, 49–54

Lori Region, *photo section*

Lumma. See "Search for a *Lumma* (Penny), The"

Lycanthropy, 42 n. *See also* "Legend about Tiridates (Trdat) III, The"

Maiden with Forty Braids, xxx. *See also* "Dzheiran-ogly, the Deer's Son"

Mamikonian, Vardan, xxii

Mamluk Kingdom, xx

Man, old. *See* "Flower of Paradise, The"

Map, of Armenia, xxxiv

Märchen. See Fairy tales

Marriage, xxiv

Marxism, xxi

Mashtots, Mesrop, xxviii, xviii fig., xxix, 37 n. *See also* "Blazing a Trail"

Masis, Mount. *See* Ararat, Mount

Massacre of Armenians, xv, xx

Massacres, genocide, and the Diaspora, xx–xxi

"Master and the Hired Man, The," xxvii, xxxi, 138–41

May 9th Victory Day, xxiv

Mazdoon, 76. *See also* "Beardless Sorcerer and the King's Son, The"

Medea, xix

Tigran (Dikran) the Great. *See* Tigranes the Great

Tigranakert, xix

Tigranes the Great, xix

Timur the Lame. *See* Tamerlane

Tiridates (Trdat) III, King, xvii, xx, 42 n, *photo section. See also* "Legend about Tiridates (Trdat) III, The"

Tobacco pouch, magic, xxx. *See also* "Peasant's Son and the King's Daughter, The"

Tonir, 105 n. *See also* "Beardless Sorcerer and the King's Son, The"; "Extraordinary Cucumber, The"; "You Reap What You Sow"

Toumanian, Hovhannes, xxvi

Traditions
applied arts and crafts, xxiv–xxv
dress, xxiv
family, xxiv
marriage, xxiv

Transcaucasian Soviet Federated Socialist Republic, xxi

Transfiguration, xxiii, xxiii fig.

Translation of tales, xxviii

Tricksters, xxviii, xxix, xxxi. *See also* Silly Pugi

Trndez. See Purification

Tsaghkazard. See Palm Sunday

Turkey, xv, xix–xxi, xxiv. *See also* Turkish and Mongol rule

Turkish and Mongol rule, xx

"Two Brothers," 158–60

"Two Foxes," xxix, 15–16

Types of the Folktale, The: A Classification and Bibliography, xxvii, xxxiv n.27

Union of Soviet Socialist Republics. *See* Soviet Union

Urartu, Kingdom of, xix

Vahan, Varbed, *photo section*

Van, Lake, xix, *photo section*

Van Fortress, *photo section*

Vardanants, xxii

Vardavar, photo section. See also Transfiguration

Victory Day, xxiii, xxiv

Vishap, 54 n. *See also* "Little Bear"

Vishhapakagh. See Carpet designs

Vizier. *See* "Beardless Sorcerer and the King's Son, The"; "Gambar"; "Invincible Rooster, The"; "Little Bear"; "Mirror, The"; "Peasant's Son and the King's Daughter, The"

Vorotan, xvi

Wand, magic. *See* "Forty Thieves"

Watermelons. *See* "Why the Onion Is Bitter"

Wedding, *photo section. See also* "Beardless Sorcerer and the King's Son, The"; "Death or Freedom"; "Extraordinary Cucumber, The"; "Pitcher of Gold, The"; "Snake Child Otsamanuk and Arevamanuk, Who Angered the Sun"; "Sparrow, The"

"When My Heart Tells Me," xxxi, 143

White Dev, xxx. *See also* "Dzheiran-ogly, the Deer's Son"; "Flower of Paradise, The"

"Why the Onion Is Bitter," xxix, 44–45

Wit, xxii, xxviii, xxx

Wits and dimwits, xxvii, xxxi
"Brother Ax," 153–54
"Carnival," 155–57
"Death or Freedom," 149
"The Donkey That Swallowed the Moon," 144
"The Golden Apple," 137
"The Master and the Hired Man," 138–41
"The Ne'er-Do-Well Son," 145–48
"Pugi and His Neighbor," 169
"Pugi and His Wife," 167
"The Raven," 168
"The Shoemaker's Debt," 142
"Silly Pugi and His Friend," 165

ABOUT THE AUTHOR

Bonnie C. Marshall—author, teacher, translator, and folklorist—is a museum teacher for the New Hampshire Historical Society. A native of New Hampshire, she received her education at Boston University, Assumption College, and the University of North Carolina, as well as from three institutions of higher learning in Russia—Moscow State University, Leningrad State University, and the Herzen Institute.

Dr. Marshall established Russian programs at Davidson College and at Johnson C. Smith University, where she served as Adjunct Associate Professor of Russian and Curriculum Coordinator of the Russian Program. She taught Russian at several universities in the United States, including the University of South Alabama, the University of Montana, and the College of the Holy Cross. In addition, Dr. Marshall taught English in St. Petersburg and Moscow at the School for Global Education and the American Academy of Foreign Languages.

Her publications include the prize-winning *Baba Yaga's Geese and Other Russian Stories* (1973) and translations of Yevgeny Ryss's *Search Behind the Lines* (1974) and Anatoli Aleksin's *Alik the Detective* (1977), *Grasshopper to the Rescue* (1979, Junior Literary Guild Award), *Tales from the Heart of the Balkans* (2001), and *The Snow Maiden and Other Russian Tales* (2004).

ABOUT THE EDITOR

Author of *Once There Was and Was Not: Armenian Tales Retold* (1966) and *Three Apples Fell From Heaven: Armenian Folk Tales Retold* (1971), as well as several other publications, **Virginia A. Tashjian** served as children's librarian and director of libraries for the city of Newton, Massachusetts, from 1970 to 1993. She taught children's literature at Simmons College Graduate School of Library and Information Science and lectured at several area colleges.

She has won awards for her librarian work and is proud of her role in the opening of a new main library in Newton, which she envisioned as a center of cultural and educational life. She was elected President of the Massachusetts Library Association and the New England Library Association.

Tashjian is a popular storyteller and lecturer. The Newton Library's Children's Room was named in her honor. She was one of two delegates representing the United States at the Third International John Masefield Storytelling Festival in Toronto.

She is a member of the Women's National Book Association, the Women's Educational and Industrial Union, the Friends of Armenian Culture Society, the Boston Symphony, the Lyric Opera Theater and Huntington Theatre in Boston, and many other organizations.

Proud of her heritage and the Armenian Church, Tashjian served as Superintendent of St. Stephen's Church Sunday School for ten years. She can speak, read, and write Armenian. Her life has been dedicated to passing on the Armenian language, culture, and values to her family and community.